A Worship Shepherd

"I first came to know and appreciate Tony as a gifted songwriter, a great communicator, and one of my favorite singers (which of course had nothing to do with the fact that he was one of the first recording artists to record one of my songs!). Then, I got to know him as a dear friend and brother, who, along with his wife Cindy, cared deeply for my young family and me at a time when we desperately needed it. Through the thirty-five-plus years I've known Tony, I have seen and heard the heart of a shepherd beat consistently and faithfully in his life. I am thankful, as I know all who read this book will be, that he has shared his wisdom and passion from his shepherd's heart!"

—**STEVEN CURTIS CHAPMAN,** Hall of Fame, Multi-Grammy and Dove Award-Winning Artist and Songwriter

"I have always loved Tony Elenburg because I've always loved his heart. *A Worship Shepherd* reveals his heart through his experience, wisdom, and faith as a Christian artist, songwriter, pastor, and worship leader. The combination is powerful and insightful for anyone pursuing the true heart of ministry! My heart beats with Tony's. These words are so much needed in reclaiming Christian music ministry for Christ's glory!"

—**SCOTT WESLEY BROWN,** Worship Leader, Dove Award-Winning Recording Artist and Songwriter

"*A Worship Shepherd* is a must-read informative for every member of any worship team. It's beautifully written and, more importantly, a Word-centered thesis that deals with every possible aspect of worship. I know Tony Elenburg as an enormously gifted musician and seasoned worship leader. His wise insights come from years of experience mentoring worship teams and caring for the congregations he leads. I highly recommend it."

—**GREG NELSON,** Multi-Grammy and
Dove Award-Winning Record Producer and Songwriter

"Tony Elenburg has a heart for ministry and those who help create it. He understands creatives and knows how to help them shape their ministry without trying to manipulate it or form it into something that fits a preconceived design. Having played worship services with Tony, and being a longtime friend, I know the heart and care he has for worship and the people who lead it."

—**PHIL NAISH,** Multi-Grammy and
Dove Award-Winning Record Producer,
Keyboard Player, and Songwriter

"At the center of our relationship with God is the essence of worship—an internal encounter that produces an external response. Tony Elenburg has given his life to understanding that heart of a worshipper. His life is the external response to an internal encounter with Christ. *A Worship Shepherd* is a life's work of discovering how to live a life of worship and help others become worshippers. It's a must-read for every heart that desires to understand what worshipping Christ can really look like."

—**DAVID VESTAL,** Author, Songwriter,
and Pastor of Gateway Church Apostolic Network

A Worship Shepherd

A Call to
Gospel-Centered Worship Ministry

Tony Elenburg

*This book is dedicated to the memory of
Charles T. Chivers:
A life well-lived.*

Contents

Introduction

The shepherd stood on an outcropping overlooking the flock, as he did for what seemed most of his existence. Though he could not see it, he knew there was an uneasiness stirring among the flock. He knew this in a way that resulted from knowing silence; not as in the absence of sound, but in a way wherein he could distinguish sounds that were not common among the flock and were not consistent with the normal movement that would accompany an evening on the plains. This solitude enabled him to separate sounds that were strange and, more importantly, unsafe.

Several times throughout the day, he counted the flock. But as the sun disappeared over the horizon, an immediate sense of danger called for a quicker and more efficient method of counting. He arose like a sentinel with a calm, controlled fierceness, as one looking out over a large family. He looked for the mature sheep, knowing their presence would most likely assure the safety of smaller groups; or, as a mother would know instinctively where her offspring would be.

Twilight, the eye's disadvantaged time between daylight and darkness, is the enemy's preferred time of assault. Time and experience have demonstrated this will be the vulnerable moments when the flock begins to graze, and the very movement itself will be the enemy's concealment from the shepherd and the flock. Those seeking to do harm to the flock were common. They were not unknown. As a matter of fact, they were well-known to the shepherd. He had been attacked so many times by these same enemies that he could identify which ones they were by the way they approached or stalked the flock. Their patterns of stalking were subtle, but predictably revealing.

The shepherd began in soft tones, so as not to panic the sheep. He calmly called his flock to move in a direction and manner they had heard many times.

Their act of compliance was the very essence that exposed the threat. Imposters were revealed not for the way they acted, but for their failure to react to the voice of the shepherd. While sheep were generally compliant and led easily, goats were rebellious. They tend not to listen to instruction and wander. "He shall set the sheep on his right hand, but the goats on the left" (Matthew 25:33, ASV). The sheep know and trust the voice of the shepherd, and as he calmly directed his flock toward safety, the imposter was exposed and decisively eliminated.

The removal of the threat was often executed with such efficiency that the flock might never have known they were being attacked.

One of the greatest needs of the contemporary church is for shepherding, mentoring, and fathering our worship and worship ministries. We value the investments of our lead pastors, those who have prepared to accurately divide the Word and responsibly shepherd our congregations; and yet, many times we have abdicated our responsibilities to worship leaders by providing little or no shepherding oversight, guidance, and protection. Many of today's worship leaders are often left to grasp and grope for their own definition of a meaningful, successful ministry of worship. And yet, our worship ministries represent 40 percent (avg) of the weekly "touchpoint" with our communities in the Sunday morning service.

To entrust the weight and responsibility of worship to those who (for no fault of their own) are unprepared shows a reckless disregard for the importance of worship (not to mention the carelessness with which we steward people).

My heart and passion is for creatives (musicians, artists). If we don't shepherd well those who are creatively gifted, the world is all too eager to offer "counterfeit carrots"—the promise of fame, fortune, recognition, and significance. All of which it portends, but most always fails to deliver. Even the most successful creatives will admit in their more reflective moments: "Success is not *at all* what I thought it would be."

I am an elder worship pastor who has lived through and experienced the Jesus Movement, the Christian Recording Artist Movement, the Worship Movement, and the Worship Artist Movement, to its current state. And through each of these eras, I have found there is simply no substitution for a gospel-centered song being sung by a gospel-centered worship leader in a gospel-centered worship service in a gospel-centered community of believers. There are few issues we face (if any) that can't be resolved by applying the transformational power of the gospel.

A Worship Shepherd will provide a foundational understanding of God's creation of music (and the arts) and how to practically apply the clarifying filter of the gospel to our worship and to the high calling of worship ministry.

CHAPTER 1

The Value of a Worship Shepherd

The following is what one pastor described as the ideal formula for a successful worship ministry: "Find the youngest musician who can sing while playing a keyboard or guitar, and let them build your worship ministry." I'm not sure if he was serious, but I would suggest the strategies for building a worship ministry may indeed have started with less thought than this. I hope he was kidding. I understand how difficult it is to find good, qualified worship leaders and pastors, but we need to take a serious and sober approach to choosing those who shepherd our hearts in worship—equally as serious, as with any other staff pastor or position.

There is an amazing crossroads of giftings a good worship leader must exhibit (many times simultaneously). But the scarcity of these multitalented leaders is not because they are rare; rather, we have been neglectful in identifying, mentoring, fathering, and calling out these young men and women and giving them a vision for their gifts and talents within the context of a worship ministry. We will visit this more extensively in Chapter 5: "A Good Worship Leader Is a Shepherd First."

Understanding Creatives

Allow me to speak for the creative camp. Creatives think outside the box. It's the nature of creativity. It's why in a staff meeting, after listening to our perspective on a matter, we often leave other staff members staring at us like a calf looking at a new gate. We can be conversation killers. (Not intentionally.) We think from the right side of the brain. Our shoptalk sounds more like air-traffic-control chatter than a normal conversation—with a mind-scrambling description of a chord pattern as DAD, GAD, 2 minor, 4 5 1! In building a worship ministry, it is important to understand creatives, their culture, and their language.

My first memories regarding my musical gifts were the love and affirmation I received from my family. How patient they were! To prove how patient my father was, he showed me a room in our detached garage where I could practice. *Wow!* I thought. *My own space!* In hindsight, maybe they weren't so excited. Seriously, my father was my number one fan, and a tremendous mentor. He was a great guitar player and had an exceptional ear for chord progression.

Eventually, for the young musician, the opportunity to perform before the family-at-large arrives. Most listen intently, but Aunt Beth talks during the whole performance. As the applause subsides, the inevitable compliment from a well-meaning family member is spoken into existence: "Wow, you're good. You should go to Nashville (or LA or Broadway)!"

There it is—the seed is planted in the young musician's psyche: *In order to be fulfilled in my musical gift, I must be validated by the music or showbiz industry. In order to be fulfilled, I must seek a much larger stage, a national stage, or perhaps a worldwide stage!* Though intended as a compliment or encouragement from family members, no single lie has misinformed musically gifted people more than this hollow and narrow vision of creative fulfillment.

If you are creative (musically or otherwise), it is so because God made it so; and as with all of His creation, it was granted for a specific and intended purpose: to Glorify God, to serve others, and to partner with God in building His kingdom. Unless the musician gets this ordered in his heart and mind, music will always be a source of frustration rather than the joy God intended.

I am not opposed to musicians using their gifts in secular or profit-motivated endeavors, provided they have wrestled with these foundational principles and are not seduced into seeking fulfillment and validation in the applause and approval of man.

It is my conviction that we need to help musicians find context for their gifts. My pursuit of the heart of God in this matter has led me to this conclusion: the highest calling God can place on a musician is to serve the church. If I could put this in a three-inch bold heading, it would not be overemphasized. It's from this foundational platform that music's created power emanates. It is the foundation from which everything flows; to operate out of the understanding and knowledge that music (in its created essence) is intended to glorify God, to serve others, and to partner with God in building His kingdom.

I refer to creatives who understand this context as "sat down" in their spirit. It's like sitting atop a spaceship launch knowing you certainly have a critical function to perform, but also knowing this vehicle is part of a grand design. And yet, in the God-created nature of music, you get to partner with God as an instrument in demonstrating its created power and purpose.

God's Design for Music and Our Gifts

Music and art are never more powerful than when they are being used for their created purpose.

When creatives have successfully ordered this in their heart, they experience validation, affirmation, fulfillment, and encouragement. These are all acceptable, God-given needs and desires. It's important to understand that these needs are not met through the music or the gifts, but rather, through God the Father, as a blessing for cooperating with His grand design for our gifts. Study the chart below to help visualize this design for music and gifts. It's foundational.

God's Design for Music and Gifts

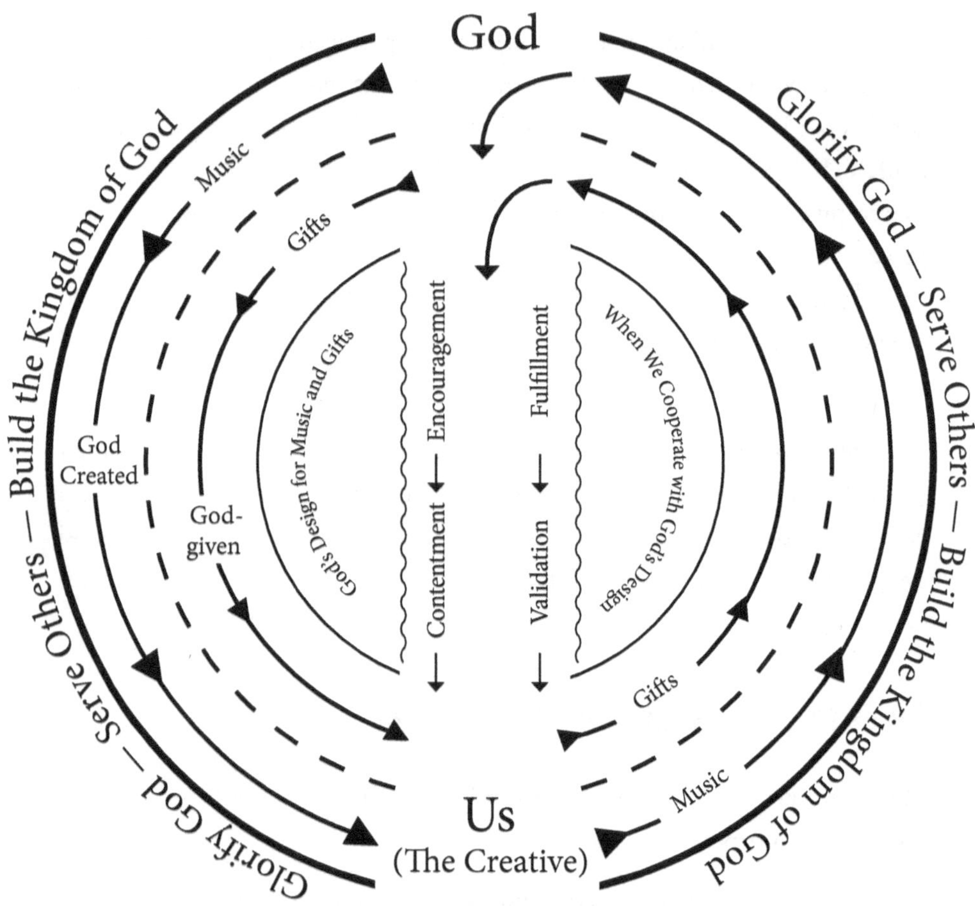

The Counterfeit

As you would expect, the enemy seeks to distract creatives with a counterfeit design for music and gifts. And those who have no concept of an intelligent, loving Creator are especially vulnerable. Rather than worshipping the Creator, the enemy substitutes the creation itself as the object of worship; thus, the music and gift become the object of worship. It is a subtle, cruel, and deceptive sleight of hand.

We see in the world many creatives who:

- use their gift for self-glorification instead of glorifying God;

- become self-serving instead of serving others; and

- build kingdoms unto themselves instead of building the kingdom of God.

I have seen this reality firsthand in my forty years in the music industry from those who (because of their success) should have every reason to feel affirmed, validated, fulfilled, and encouraged. But we would be wrong to assume.

Here's a disturbing observation of my industry: Nashville is full of gifted, talented, successful, and depressed people. What's wrong with that statement? Do all those adjectives belong in the same sentence? Sadly, in many cases, yes. Success can be quite depressing when, after climbing the ladder of success, the reality does not match the anticipated fulfillment. Study the counterfeit below.

The Counterfeit

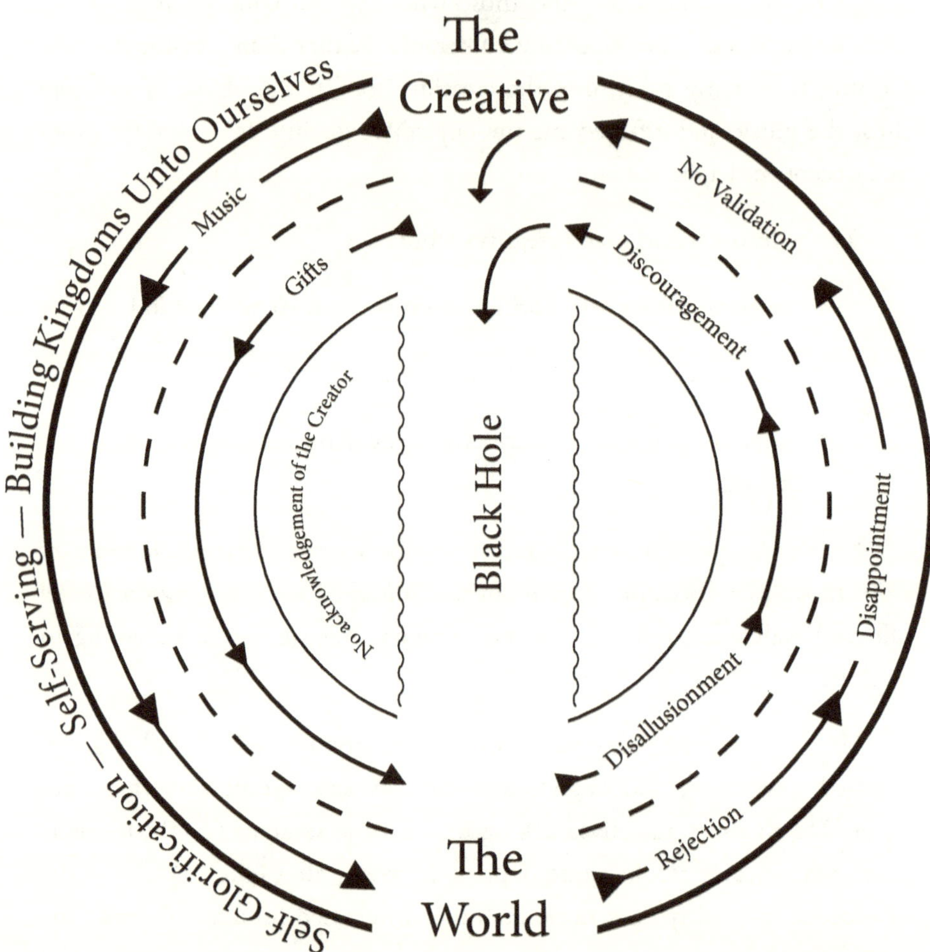

Allow this proportion to my previous statement: While Nashville is full of many who exhibit an unhealthy orphan-type spirit (a foundational misunderstanding of our relationship status with God) regarding their gifts, Nashville is also full of wonderful, gifted people who represent the balance and hope of the gospel to the music industry on a regular basis. Many of these are successful secular musicians and artists, so I am not suggesting one must represent only Christian music to have ordered these priorities. Some have managed to artfully navigate a somewhat foreign culture with the wisdom of the gospel. I love these lifelong friends and pray for them often. But they, too, would agree that there are far too many who, through no fault of their own, have no context for their gifts and talents.

For obvious reasons of clarity and understanding, I would like to elaborate and illustrate my use of this phrase "orphan spirit," which I use many times in this book. This story has likely been retold in thousands of adoptive homes throughout the world but will serve as a clear illustration of the orphan spirit:

There was a young couple who had attempted unsuccessfully to conceive a child and had decided to adopt. They completed the long adoption process and were to receive two sisters from an adoption agency in China. They traveled to China to gather their new family. As they prepared to leave the orphanage and return home, they drove to an airport to board a plane back to America. As you might imagine, the couple's attention was completely transfixed on their new daughter's comfort and experience for the journey home. They noticed the sisters' astonishment at the whole airport and airplane experience, realizing each experience and sight was a first and new adventure for these young children. Landing in America, they saw roads intertwined in a confusing yet amazing display of order. They saw homes more grand (by comparison) than anything they had ever seen before. They stood in wonder in the foyer of their new home, then each were shown rooms that were to be their very own (not having to share with one another anymore). They were shown closets and dressers full of clothes, just their size—cleaned, pressed, and awaiting their use. They were shown a pantry stocked to the ceiling and a refrigerator stocked with more food than seemed possible to consume.

Life was certainly different for these two girls who had never seen such abundance. So much so that it was hard to grasp the good fortune they had been swept into.

One day, as the mother was returning clothes to the dressers after washing, she was confused to find food stuffed and hidden in the deep corners of the drawers. After a discussion with the father, they realized the young daughters were having difficulty comprehending the grace that had been extended to them as daughters in the house! Though they were no longer orphans, they were still living out of an old nature. A nature that informed them that this grace was temporary, or motivated by their performance, perhaps.

The father, wanting very much to assure them of his love and acceptance, walked them to the pantry and, with a wave of his hand, said, "Everything you see here is yours! Everything I have is yours! You are our daughters, and this home is yours."

What a heartwarming scene this is. And yet, we as sons and daughters of God often (even after we are secure in our salvation) still live with an orphan mentality that tells us God's love and acceptance of us is only temporary. It whispers that "if I don't perform, or earn my salvation, God will reject me. After all, others have."

The truth is, it's not within our mind's ability to understand the boundless limits of God's love and grace toward us. We are no longer orphans, but sons and daughters. In my own experience as a father, I have only to look at my own children to understand the permanence of my love and grace toward them; yet, how much more is God's ability to love and accept them?

If you are born again and have received into your heart the fullness of the work of Christ on the cross, you are no longer an orphan. You are a son or daughter of God! You are coheirs with Christ—of the inheritance of the kingdom of God! You are a member of God's family (because of Jesus). You are free to glorify God, to serve others, and to invest your gifts and talents in building the kingdom of God, You are no longer an orphan!

A Healthy Foundation

There is no more all-encompassing demonstration of the power of music than when someone is "sat down" in the full anointing and understanding of their gift. And there is no more powerful demonstration for our congregations than to be in a room full of creatives (musicians and technical artists) who understand their role in bringing their gifts to the table for the benefit of the entire body. What better example of Paul's exhortation in Romans 12:5–6 (ESV): "So we, though many, are one body in Christ, and individually members one of another. Having gifts that differ according to the grace given to us . . ." Every Sunday, the worship ministry is a living example of the body of Christ when each member brings their voice, instrument, or technical gift to worship for one unified purpose.

A healthy gospel-informed foundation for worship ministry should reflect a love for people and be every bit as much of an outreach as any other element of the church. Our vision for building a worship team should be to engage as many people as possible. Choirs (plural intended), orchestras, multiple worship teams, multiple youth worship teams, singles-ministry worship teams, and, in a COVID world, an increasing demand for those who can lead worship in small-group settings, to name but a few.

A primary goal is relationship and influence—by any and all means. Worship should not merely be the musical expression of the church; it should be a means of fulfilling the Great Commission: "Go therefore and make disciples of all nations, baptizing them in the name of the Father and of the Son and of the Holy Spirit, teaching them to observe all that I have commanded you. And behold, I am with you always, to the end of the age" (Matthew 28:19–20, ESV).

Some of the greatest opportunities to share my passion and faith was in a room full of musicians who had been drawn together because of our common love for music. I liken it as unto a campfire: the music draws us to its warmth, its light, its refuge, and our common love and need for it. It's where creatives more willingly listen to the clarifying origins of their gifts and the purposes God intended for music. And these were times I discovered my love of pastoring creatives.

One motivation for wanting to use choirs and orchestras in our worship (in addition to the awesome dynamic they bring) is to give a larger group of people the opportunity to experience healthy community. I would often troll my congregation for people with musical or technical gifts; not only for the benefit to the worship ministry, but because I was eager to help people find community and a context for their gift. If I could build ten worship teams, I would. If I encountered enough string players (violins, violas, cellos, bassists), I would suggest God is providing an orchestra. It is my conviction that if God dispensed these gifts, He had a plan for these gifts.

In my travels, I would see old friends, some of whom were musically gifted (some incredibly so). I would ask if they were involved with their worship ministry, to which many replied, "Well, no, not at the moment. I just haven't found the right time to plug in." To which I would walk them straight to the worship pastor and make an introduction. I want the church to receive the blessing of the musician, but I also want the musician to find the fulfillment of using their gifts for the high and noble calling of serving the church.

In my search for meaning and purpose regarding my own gifts, I genuinely searched the heart of God with this question: "Why, God, would you gift so many people creatively when so few ever find fulfillment in their gift?"

To which I felt God replied simply, "And why would I?"

The unpacked explanation is as follows: The gospel of Jesus Christ is (among many things) a filter through which we separate truth from lie. It is the reality of life for which Christ was born, lived, died, and was resurrected. Of the many implications of the gospel, it restores order in our thinking. The gospel-ordered heart and mind inform us that when we seek fulfillment in the creation rather than through the Creator, we inevitably settle for the counterfeit, which, ironically in this case, can be in the gift itself. The gift was not given to simply fulfill us; it was given primarily to glorify God, to serve others, and to partner with God to build His kingdom.

As we cooperate with God's design for our gifts, we receive all our heart's desire as creatives: fulfillment, validation, and encouragement—not from the gift, but from God.

In I Samuel 16:14–23, we find Saul tormented by troubling spirits. But when David served him by playing his harp, it brought great peace to Saul. I'm sure there were other available harpists, but I believe David's music was especially comforting because he had "sat down in his spirit" regarding his gift. God's presence inhabited His creation of music, and David was the instrument through which it was delivered. David had ordered his heart and his role regarding his gift of music.

This ordered heart for musicians is a subtle state of posture before the Lord, but it's the difference between noise and the life-giving manifest presence of God in our music and art.

A Shepherd's Thoughts

Good mentoring and fathering involve long obedience in the same direction, with wisdom and instruction consistently applied. Proverbs 4:7 (ESV) says: "The beginning of wisdom is this: Get wisdom, and whatever you get, get insight."

When my son was about two years old, he had a love of seedless grapes. We were more than happy to always have his favorite snack on hand. Until he developed the curious and random habit of disposing the stems into the toe of our shoes (consistently). Without instruction, this solution seemed reasonable to his two-year-old mind: "Here's a convenient place to rid myself of these tasteless and unpleasant grape holders."

My wife Cindy began giving him the grapes in a bowl and taught him to put the stems in the trash when he was finished. Problem solved, right? We were happy when we began finding the stems in the trash, but the stems were in the bowls. He was throwing the stems away *with* the bowls. With time and patience, he eventually got it right: stem in the trash, bowl on the counter. We knew his desire was obedience, but our instruction lacked his young perspective.

I am an elder creative who understands the difficulty young creatives experience in navigating and reconciling their gifts with their calling. I have experienced this journey in my own life. Many of those I have had the privilege of pastoring and mentoring have far exceeded anything I will ever accomplish or experience, and it's extremely satisfying. But I truly believe they have largely succeeded because they have effectively applied the filter of the gospel to their gifts, their art, and their ministries.

The common unifying theme of the following chapters is the gospel. When we learn to see our gifts, art, worship, and worship ministries through a gospel lens, we will see that Jesus has left a clear and meaningful context for our gifts and art—and a template for our worship and worship ministries.

If you are a creative (young or old), lean in to this teaching. It is a foundation that will inform you and the thousands of decisions you will need to make for the rest of your life. My confidence is not in my teaching or communicating, but in the foundational and transformational power of the gospel.

The foundation for a beautiful and productive garden is the soil (the tilling). It's mostly hard work (I've planted many gardens). But when the soil is prepared well, the water finds and nourishes the seed, and the garden yields a great harvest. The harvest not only blesses you, but it can also feed many others, who come to partake of the bounty.

You can do this! I'm praying for you.

CHAPTER 2

Man Was Created to Worship . . . and He Does!

W e worship whether we are conscious of our actions or not. We either choose whom we worship, or it is chosen for us. Man was created to worship. And he does! Though most may not identify their lives as an expression of worship.

Allow me to unpack these statements with an illustration: I have long been known to binge-watch *The Andy Griffith Show*. Oh, I assure you, I know every line of every episode. You're probably wondering, "What, pray tell, does Andy Griffith have to do with worship?" Hang with me, I'm going somewhere with this!

I think this TV series represents a historically rare combination of writing and talent that touches an innate yearning within the human heart. It fills a curious longing in me for things that are simple, safe, and predictable. But interestingly, somewhere in my experience, the entertainment value of the show ceased to be my motivation for watching. I found myself watching (and sometimes simply listening) for reasons other than entertainment; like familiar voices and values that affirmed my own. I like it because it reminds me of home. The Taylor front porch represents community, family, identity, and belonging.

God has created an innate desire within us for *home*, and all it represents (whether it was a good experience, or only in our imaginations): comfort, peace, acceptance, belonging, security, contentment, and much more. And we learn in John 14:2–4 (ESV) where our ultimate home is. Jesus said:

> In my Father's house are many rooms. If it were not so, would I have told you that I go to prepare a place for you? And if I go and prepare a place for you, I will come again and will take you to myself, that where I am you may be also. And you know the way to where I am going."

Ultimately, Jesus is home. *He* is the place our hearts long for; where we experience comfort, peace, acceptance, belonging, security, contentment, fulfillment—all that calls to us, all the yearnings of our heart. God the Father is home. God the Father is the object of our worship.

Have you ever revisited a house you once lived in? Perhaps a house from your youth? Maybe you walked the halls and rooms that were once filled with the voices and sounds that made it home. Did you experience the twinge of longing for the way it once was? I believe God has placed this yearning in our hearts, for home, and all it represents. In this yearning He calls to us!

As a pastor, I have heard stories from many wounded people and have seen the destruction that sin has wrought upon the homes and childhoods of people I love. These precious people don't have good memories of home. It breaks my heart. But one of the greatest benefits of a gospel-centered church family is to replace the hope of home with one that reclaims the acceptance, love, and identity that has been stolen. Perhaps this is you. If so, let God have those empty corners of your heart. He can perfectly replace what was stolen from you. I pray that the Lord will grant grace and restoration to you.

The central yearning of the human heart (believer and nonbeliever) is an innate desire for God (home). We were created to long for God the Father. Worship is the activity God has created to experience His presence. When man does not recognize this innate yearning and design, he seeks to fill his need for worship with unhealthy pursuits in an attempt to fill the need: perhaps a pursuit of success, fame, wealth, or power (however defined). And whatever is perceived to be a requirement to attain this end becomes a substitutionary object of worship. Man was created to worship. And he does! I Corinthians 2:14 (ESV) says, "The natural person does not accept the things of the Spirit of God, for they are folly to him, and he is not able to understand them because they are spiritually discerned."

Worship is God's provision for our innate need of Him and His presence. The counterfeit is the consequence of misdirected worship:

- To a natural man, the pursuit of the *security* of home might lead him to worship money.

- To a natural man, the pursuit of the *acceptance* of home might lead him to worship fame.

- To a natural man, the pursuit of the *belonging* of home might lead him to the worship of man.

Though the natural man's worship is misdirected, make no mistake: he does worship.

This is, in essence, why man is prone to worship the creation rather than the Creator. Man, void of the counsel of the Holy Spirit, will likely worship only what he can see, touch, or experience; he lacks the spiritual or dimensional capacity to recognize spiritual realities and/or the hand of the Creator.

In the 1980s, stereograms became very popular. I first saw them as posters hanging in malls, where they usually attracted a rather intense and serious crowd. These stereograms were a computer-generated image giving a three-dimensional representation of a solid object or surface, which, upon first glance, did not seem to make much sense. For a time, I could never see the image others swore they could see! I thought it was another snipe hunt hoax; I was convinced, as I stared cross-eyed into the confusing maze, that my friends were all behind me slapping their knees and laughing.

But one day it happened. As if by magic, another dimension suddenly appeared, and I saw its depth and wonder. Apparently, it had been there all the time, but until I allowed my mind's eye to adjust to that reality, I did not see it.

In much the same way, when we worship, we are allowing time for the eyes of our heart to awaken and align with the spiritual reality that exists all around us.

God is spirit, and those who worship him must worship in spirit and truth.

—JOHN 4:24 (ESV)

Worship in Our Music

It's important to have a universal understanding of worship (worship in the Word, worship in our giving, worship in our serving, and worship in our sacraments). But in the current contemporary church, *worship* is most often used to identify the music element of our church services. The current vernacular identifies music as *the worship*. While we want to be accurate in our representation of all aspects of the universal concept of worship, I will be unpacking worship in the context of music for the purposes of this book. We will use *music, worship, congregational singing* interchangeably, but they will all be intended as a general discussion of *the worship service.*

Though congregational singing is only one of many expressions of a universal understanding of worship, the benefits to the world and the kingdom of God are multifaceted and significant, both in this world and in eternity:

- It is the source of great joy, peace, and comfort to the human soul and spirit (Psalm 100:1–2).

- It is a great witness to the world (Acts 2:6).

- It is an excellent means of promoting unity among the body of Christ (Psalm 133:1).

- It is the activity here on earth that most mimics eternity (past, present, and future) (Psalm 107).

- It is the time in which we allow the Holy Spirit to tune our hearts to the *true reality* that exists all around us (the spiritual dimension) (John 4:23).

A Shepherd's Thoughts

Worship is more than a prelude to the message. It fills a desperate need in our hearts to connect with home. Home is the safe place where you are loved unconditionally. Home is where we receive deposits in our *emotional and spiritual bank accounts*, when the world has been unkind and has made unauthorized withdrawals. It is where we are picked up, brushed off, and set again on our feet to face life with a sense of identity and belonging; a place that affirms our value and recenters our priorities. We all need to visit home more often than we realize.

Keith and Kristyn Getty (Sing) provide this clarifying and affirming description of all that is taking place when we sing together:

> All our individual stories meet at the cross-section of the worship service. We are reminded that we are not alone—we are members of a multi-generational, multi-ethnic, multi-everything family. We are reminded that we are not self-sufficient, for we need a Savior. We are reminded that we need not despair, for we have His Spirit within us. We are reminded that we are not the center of the universe, but just one voice and heart among the great worldwide throng of people praising the One who is. And, we remind each other of all this as we sing—together.[1]

Pray this prayer:

God grant us spiritual eyes to see what is taking place in the moments we are leading worship. Give us a sensitivity to the importance of the communion we are serving between the bride and the bridegroom. Give us the heart of a shepherd with the love and sensitivity to the need of the moment. Make us aware we are standing with a myriad

---

1 Keith and Kristyn Getty, *Sing: How Worship Transforms Your Life, Family, and Church* (Nashville: B&H Publishing Group, 2017), pg. 79. Permission granted.

of people, angels, and hosts of heaven, that we are joining in with a song that has been sung in Heaven for eternity—such that John describes in Revelation 5 as a sight and sound so glorious as to have driven the elders to their knees time and again! And they've never seen the same thing twice! Give us this awareness of the awesome privilege of leading others in worship of the King of Kings and Lord of Lords. Amen.

CHAPTER 3

The Vision, Mission, and Values of a Healthy Worship Ministry

I remember when I was first asked to create vision, mission, and values statements. The thought of this exercise did not interest me in the least. It was only when I was heart-deep into leading people that I learned of its immense value. These ministry principles are the corner posts of worship ministry. *Vision* is a description of where you are going, and what you seek to be and do; *mission* is the strategy you intend to employ to fulfill the vision; and *values* are the statements of nonnegotiable principles that guide and inform the process of building and maintaining the vision and mission. I learned to appreciate these, not unlike a pair of glasses I had to wear each morning; in order to function with clarity, I had to first see my day through the filter of the vision, the mission, and the values we embrace.

Getting these principles in order is foundational. I was born in Texas but spent a significant part of my youth in Montana. When my family moved from Texas to Montana, my father, who grew up on a farm in Texas, wanted to reconnect with his past by investing in some land and cattle. In those years, my father experimented with the idea of making me a rancher. The experiment didn't work. I had my sights set on a career in music, and Nashville was calling to me like a fat kid to a cupcake. I was convinced ranching in Montana was a dead end. Ironically, I discovered the motivation for success (according to many in the recording industry) was the dream of owning a ranch in Montana.

Wait . . . what?

I had a vision for what I wanted to do (music), but apparently, I had not thought it through as thoroughly as I should have. Or those who dreamed of owning a ranch in Montana had never experienced the more pungent end of a cow. So, vision should be an important priority.

Embrace Who You Are

I am occasionally asked, "What should a vision for worship ministry look like?" There's not a one-size-fits-all vision for worship. There are unique realities that should inform your ministry principles. Most churches have vision and mission statements. If not, that would be a first step before you can effectively establish the same for your worship ministry, because the worship vision and mission should likewise serve and complement the vision and mission of the church.

During World War II, I'm sure the vision and mission were along these lines: Win the war, restore order to the nations, as expediently and economically as possible, and bring home our troops with as few casualties as possible. I'm relatively sure it wasn't necessary to remind the generals and admirals of this overarching vision at every meeting. But it was there, and with little discussion, it served as a common vision that served the millions of decisions necessary to execute the mission.

This being understood, the war in Europe was quite different from the war in North Africa or Italy, or more still, than the Pacific. While they all served the same overarching vision of victory, they each required different strategies, which were employed because their battlegrounds were vastly different.

All considered, our vision and mission should reflect our "battlefield." Our strategies and methods should be somewhat unique to the realities of our communities. If your church is located in the backwoods of Kentucky, and you are surrounded by bluegrass musicians, I would expect you would have the best bluegrass worship in America. Go with it! Embrace it! Celebrate it! God said, "He inhabits the praises of His people," (Psalm 22:3, paraphrased) not the style of music, nor the flawlessness of the presentation.

I like country music, but it's not my favorite style of music. Though, if I were pastoring in a rural area surrounded by country musicians, I would make every effort to engage and involve these musicians in our expression of worship, and work to have a great country worship team. Embrace the resources and people God brings. Our culture is desperate for the reality of who God is, in the most authentic, undistracted environment you can provide. Paul said: "To the weak I became weak, that I might win the weak. I have become all things to all people, that by all means I might save some. I do it all for the sake of the gospel, that I may share with them in its blessings" I Corinthians 9:22–23 (ESV).

Your vision, mission, and values statements should be a cooperative and cumulative expression of your leadership. But let this general counsel guide you: *be who you are!* People will respond to your spirit of authenticity before the Lord more than the flawlessness of your presentation and production. Most church leaders will acknowledge this as truth, but it often gets lost in the doing. The most common distraction from this truth is the constant comparison with other, larger fellowships.

I learned this principle in Nashville as a recording artist: *be good at being you.* Often, people would comment to me, "You sound like Kenny Rogers!" It was intended as a compliment, and though flattering, in the greater consideration of artistry, you really don't want to be another version of an already successful artist or songwriter. Trust me, it's not the intent of a true artist.

Don't misunderstand: I am not promoting exclusiveness for the sake of marketability, or how to make your church more appealing than the one down the street, but rather, to resist the shallow, contrived, and artificial temptation to be something you are not. And more so, to miss the opportunity to walk in the destiny and calling God has for you (as an individual and a church).

Some well-known examples of high-profile, successful worship ministries are Hillsongs and Gateway. When we visit a worship ministry that is dynamic, the good and proper response is to celebrate (with them) what God is doing. The sound God is making in that house is apparently crystal clear and dynamic. And we hope and pray it is theologically sound and meeting the needs of the community at large. But be aware: most often the reason a worship ministry is effective and dynamic is because someone had the foresight to mine some deep places and to discover the heart of God regarding their community and church.

Here are some questions you might seek answers to before formulating your ministry principles:

- What is unique about my church? What "harvest field" has God called us to occupy in this community? Maybe you are located in a small town with a large university, which causes attendance to fluctuate seasonally. How does your vision accommodate this changing dynamic? How does your mission provide relevant and effective ministry to both the college and permanent community?

- What is the life message and passion of our lead pastor? What are his convictions for ministry? What is the heart and vision of the elders?

- What is the greatest need of our community? What is the history of our community? This is important to know for older and more established communities that have a long history.

- What style of music do our musicians do well? How does God manifest Himself in our worship? Make sure your vision, mission, and values reflect the realities of your team and your congregation. Remember, a primary filter of gospel-centered worship is serving the congregation and the communion between the bride and the bridegroom.

The answers to these questions will provide depth, breadth, and power to your vision, mission, and values statements.

Avoid Mere Imitation

Effective and dynamic worship is not simply in the ability to reproduce a look or sound; it is the result of a disciplined pursuit of an authentic expression of worship. Today's seekers are desperate for an honest and genuine worship experience. You must avoid the trappings of mere imitation.

Imitating a dynamic worship ministry is good to a point, but excellent worship ministry is hard work. My career as a recording artist taught me that what separates great artists from good artists is often the patience required to do the work of excellence. And as it relates to our churches: Good ministry is not the byproduct of a big church. Rather, a big church is often the byproduct of good ministry. Good is always harder to build, but more resilient and dynamic in the long run.

As an elder at my church, I always represented this order when I sensed the "numbers metric" being used as a motivation for a decision. I have no aversion to having a large church, but we can't be motivated by numbers. We end up making too many compromises to the unique vision and values of our fellowship. We need to focus on the quality of our ministry and let God determine the size of our church.

Greg Nelson was a songwriting mentor (he was also my publisher and executive producer) who not only taught me about songwriting, but he was a big part of my development as an artist. One day in a meeting, he said something that took me years to unpack but has served me well in artistry and ministry. He said, "You focus on the depth of your ministry, and let God determine the breadth of your ministry." This subtle difference in focus has informed so much of my vision for my music, my ministry, and as a pastor of worship ministry.

Don't settle for a shadow of someone else's anointing. Your vision, mission, and values should be a unique expression of the body of Christ, which needs to be nurtured, cultivated, and celebrated.

Vision Statement

A vision statement should be an overarching, all-encompassing statement of where you are going and what you seek to be and do. I recommend you keep this statement as brief as possible; this allows it to be more easily taught, remembered, and repeated. You can provide additional documentation for the purposes of unpacking this statement as part of your literature, but keep the vision statement concise. Here are examples of vision statements:

> *Our worship ministry exists to foster and nurture God-focused, God-centered, God-exalting worship within gospel-centered community.*
>
> *The heart of our ministry is to cultivate an environment where people encounter the powerful and transforming presence of God through worship.*
>
> *Our worship ministry exists to establish and encourage a meeting place with God to experience deep, meaningful, soul-washing worship for the glory of God.*

Here's a helpful formula to get you started:

> Our worship ministry seeks to _________________ [what does it seek to be and do?] for _______________ [what kind of community?].

Mission Statement

A mission statement should express the strategy you intend to employ to fulfill the vision of worship. A mission statement should be more expansive. There is a dual responsibility in worship ministry:

1. to foster an environment for our congregations to have an encounter with God; and

2. to nurture and pastor the worship team.

The goals are mostly common between the two, but the strategies are different.

For example, we want to promote among our congregation the value of authentic, spirit-led, soul-washing abandonment in worship; and while we coach our worship teams of the same value (because they have need of the same), we have to reinforce the importance of having sufficient meaningful worship times during the week (before they come to the platform), as leading worship requires a shepherding awareness. Here are examples of a mission statement:

> *We purpose to fulfill the vision of worship by establishing qualified teams of musicians, vocalists, and technical personnel who can authentically and effectively model and impart both the heart and activity of gospel-centered worship in a way that encourages others to experience and embrace intimacy with God.*

> *We purpose to fulfill the vision of worship by accurately lifting (raising) the standard of Jesus Christ in our worship and creative arts by fostering an environment that allows others to have an encounter with God.*

> *We purpose to fulfill the vision of worship by nurturing a community of artists who value character, integrity, humility, and authenticity.*

Here's a helpful formula to get you started:

Our purpose is to ___________________ [strategy you intend to employ] to fulfill ___________________ [specific vision of worship].

Values Statement

A statement of values is one of the most useful tools for promoting a healthy and secure worship culture. Many creatives struggle to experience intimacy, and more so intimacy in community. After all, one motivation for immersing ourselves in the creative arts is (sometimes) to avoid the uncomfortableness of relationships and community. But God has designed us to live not as an island, but in community.

We find value and context for our gifts in a community of believers who share not only the same love of creative artistry, but also one that genuinely values the individual. It is a chance to experience community in a new and healthy way—the way God intended. Our identity is secure not because of our gift, but because we are sons and daughters of God. When we are tempted to seek our identity in accomplishments or gifts, community provides proportion and persepective.

In the late '80s and early '90s I had songs that were played broadly on Christian radio. It was always flattering and encouraging when people recognized my work. Inasmuch as I have settled the matter of needing recognition and affirmation from my gift, it's still satisfying when someone acknowledges my work. One night, following a concert, a young lady complimented me for my "nice presentation" and in her last parting compliment said, "And you sound just like the guy who sings that on the radio!" I was suddenly aware of my facial expression straining to maintain a smile as she walked away. My soundman and keyboard player (my community) had a good knee-slapping laugh! My value and identity were tested in that moment; as I watched, my community provided perspective for me. I soon found myself laughing with them . . . laughing at me.

The following are some examples of a statement of values (these should remain open-ended):

We value the musician more than the music.

We value character and integrity above talent and gifting.

We value our stage as a platform for ministry and influence, not a pedestal for performance.

We value and respect our team members (including tech!).

We value and respect our leaders.

We value the trust conferred upon us by the leadership of this church.

We value servanthood.

Make values a part of your vocabulary. Values must be spoken early and often to your leadership and team. Example: "Because we value the musician more than the music, we will choose to walk with him through this difficult season." Or, "Because we value servanthood over performance, we will choose a more congregational-friendly melody." Demonstrate how your values inform every aspect of your worship ministry.

You celebrate what you value, and you value what you celebrate.

As a leader, these principles will serve you well. On one occasion, our worship team was relaxing in the green room between services when a discussion arose regarding one of our vocalists (who was not present) who was struggling with her intonation (pitch). Another vocalist said, "I just turn her down in my mixer" (as each person on the platform had a personal mixer). I realized this was not consistent with the values we embrace. This discussion provided an opportunity to apply our values. I said, "You know, I think we all struggle with intonation from time to time. I know I do when I can't hear myself well. Maybe one of you could help her with her mix before the next service?" My response demonstrated our value of serving one another and respecting other team members. This exchange generated several discussions with individuals over the next few days, which offered additional opportunity to reinforce our values.

A Shepherd's Thoughts

My good friend and mentor, Kenny Thacker, taught our leadership this concept and value of common and clearly communicated ministry principles. The desired goal of effective vision, mission, and values statements is cohesion (refer to the graphic below). When these ministry principles are:

- Common yet vague, the result is confusion;

- Vague and diverse, the result is disagreement;

- Clear yet diverse, the result is division; and

- Common and clear, the result is cohesion (the desired result).

Vision, Mission, and Values

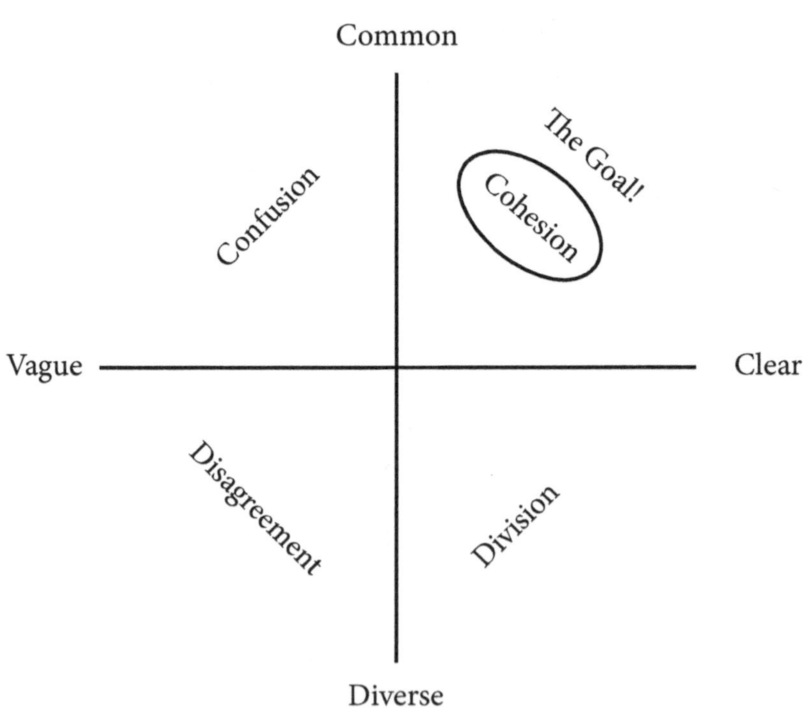

Clear and common ministry principles provide a safe and secure environment for creatives. Creativity will flourish in a community where:

- people are valued as a member of the family of God;

- order and consistency are honored; and

- everyone contributes to the common and clear vision within the context of healthy, edifying relationships.

One of my dearest friends and mentors is a man named Eddie Blakely (a great pastor, worship pastor, singer, songwriter, mentor, father, and brother). We have done life together for most of fifty years. Eddie is responsible for inspiring hundreds of men and women to the ministry of the gospel. And he quietly fathers and mentors many of them. Eddie is a quiet, introspective type and is the most patient listener I have ever known. I'm sure I've tested the limits of his patience many times. He provides a safe place for me to be me.

I did a few concerts at his church over the years, and on one such occasion, I arranged extra days to spend with him—no agenda—just to be in his world and see what he did. On a midweek day, he had a choir practice (around midmorning). We met about six senior citizens in the choir room, and they gathered chairs around a piano and Eddie led them in about seven or eight hymns. He never stopped to correct notes, improve the presentation, or tell someone they were flat. They just sang loud, and with great gusto!

After about an hour, we visited, they hugged, and everyone went on their way.

Afterward, I had an exchange with Eddie:

Me: So, that senior choir . . . do they sing in the services?
Eddie: No.

Me: Never?
Eddie: No.

Me: Do they ever sing a special in the service?
Eddie: No.

Me: Do they ever sing in the community? Like a senior center?
Eddie: No.

Me (pausing): So, why do you rehearse with them every week?
Eddie: Because they love to sing about Jesus, and I love them. And
         I think Jesus loves it too.

This is the work of excellent worship ministry: planting the seeds of value in God's people. Everything else you do should come out of this simple posture of heart: love God, love people. Let your vision, mission, and values be filtered through these primary lenses.

As you begin your process of establishing vision, mission, and values statements, the most important thing you can do is get quiet and be still before God and ask Him to give you the words and thoughts to express the heart of God in the matter of worship and worship ministry.

CHAPTER 4

The Ideal Structure for Worship Ministry

The reason for the use of *ideal* in the title acknowledges that many churches are operating under less-than-ideal realities. I realize not all churches have the luxury of a multilevel worship structure, but I recommend these roles and responsibilities be included in any vision for building and sustaining a healthy worship ministry. Regardless of available staff, consider using this as a template for growth. The larger the fellowship and worship ministry, the more critical this structure becomes.

Elder Oversight

In a biblical context, eldership is God's plan for leading the church. Biblical elders are chosen for their proven godly character and integrity and marked by their humility, servanthood, leadership skills, and their love and care for the people. A good elder smells like the sheep because his love and care for the flock often finds him among them. He has a good sense of the needs of the congregation—physical, emotional, and spiritual. This makes him an essential and valuable voice and counsel in the structure of effective worship ministry.

Identify an elder to oversee the worship ministry (preferably one who is musical and has a heart for worship). Because he is an elder, he should have a working and intimate grasp of the overarching vision and mission of the church, which will make him a valuable voice in influencing the same for the worship ministry. This will also make him an important sounding board and uplink for the worship leadership. Like the hand on the rudder of a large ship, his adjustments are minimal but critical to the outcome. His primary role is to provide a thirty-thousand-foot-level oversight to assure the worship ministry is serving the vision, mission, and values of the worship ministry and the church and to serve as counsel and encouragement to the worship leadership. His charge and focus should be big picture.

Worship Pastor

Let me make a distinction between a worship leader and a worship pastor. While on Sunday morning you might not recognize the difference between the two, there is a significant distinction. A worship pastor, like an elder, would be someone who carries the vision and values of your worship ministry, but also has a passion and heart to shepherd. The worship pastor is the day-to-day office presence and typically the liaison to the general staff.

There are dual responsibilities in a worship ministry:

1. to shepherd the congregation; and

2. to shepherd the worship team.

A worship pastor should be someone who has "sat down in their spirit" (see Chapter 1: Understanding Creatives) regarding the issues of servanthood and performance. One of the essential elements of pastoring musicians is helping them find a context for their gift (which is to glorify God). The saying is appropriate: "You cannot lead others where you yourself have not been." If we are leading others to wrestle with an orphan spirit, then we need to have wrestled with our own orphan tendencies and have thoroughly reconciled God's intended purpose for music and gifting.

Also, a good worship pastor does not need to be the only (or best) worship leader in the house, but he should be able to lead by example, on and off the platform.

Worship Leader

A worship leader is entrusted to determine a worship service set list, organize and schedule the team, rehearse the team, and lead (or conduct) the worship service (best with the advice and counsel of the worship pastor). In Chapter 5, I will explain the tremendous crossroads of giftings that are required to effectively lead a congregation. This is truly a gift, and those who are called to do so often make it appear effortless; however, it's anything but. Of the many sensitivities required, they must assure a continuity and flow for the worship service.

As I shared at the beginning of this chapter, many churches cannot afford the luxury of a worship pastor *and* a worship leader. This is not to say worship leaders are inferior; it is simply a unique skill set. There are many who lead worship with great understanding and sensitivity, but it doesn't follow that they will have a pastoral gear (gift). And, too, a worship leader who exhibits a pastoral passion does not automatically make them the best worship leader in the house. Where necessity and budget have often forced these roles into one person, they are distinct and different gifts.

This is a fine point to worship ministry, but if you're fortunate enough to have both in the house, consider allowing them each to operate in their gifting. Simply, don't force a preconceived notion that when you have one (a worship leader), you automatically have the other (a worship pastor) when they may not be ideally gifted to do both.

Song Leader

This is a *category* of worship leader—someone who may exhibit the potential to one day be a worship leader and/or worship pastor. We invite the song leader to lead a song in the worship set but would not ask them to shoulder the burden of leading an entire worship service. I have used this designation as an opportunity for training worship leaders. After a comfortable period, I might approach a song leader and suggest, "This week, when you lead your song, take your liberties to exhort the congregation, or read a passage of Scripture." Here, too, a song leader is not inferior to a worship leader or pastor but may have various qualities that justify this designation (e.g., a beautiful voice combined with an understanding of worship, a valuable testimony among the congregation, a motherly/fatherly spirit, a potential worship leader/pastor).

Counsel for Young Worship Leaders

My daughter Tori began leading worship with our youth worship team. The elders and pastors recognized, even at a young age, that she was leading with uncommon understanding and confidence. We increasingly invited her to the adult service platform. We have always utilized our youth musicians in our main services because it served our vision for multigenerational teams. Not to mention, the youth felt more connected to the larger fellowship when they saw representatives of their generation contributing. But Tori was soon invited to a regular rotation of vocalists and leaders (she also plays acoustic guitar).

As the worship pastor (and sensitive to the perceptions of favoritism), I was especially cautious of inviting Tori to our main platform. It was the request (or insistence) of David Vestal (the lead pastor) that Tori not only be invited to the platform, but that she be given a prominent role as one of our worship leaders.

Tori was a dream to coach and mentor as a worship leader. She absorbed every nuance of every counsel we had for her. Her questions were multilayered. She wanted to know the *how*, but because she sought understanding, she asked the *why*. In time, her gift was outpacing her age. David and I gave her the time to let these elements find their equilibrium before conferring upon her the burden of carrying an entire service until she was ready.

One particular recommendation we had for Tori in this season (and for any *young* worship leader who is asked to lead a multigenerational congregation) was to keep her exhortations vertical (talking or praying to God, rather than horizontally to the congregation). Like so:

> Horizontal Exhortation (directed to the congregation): *"When you and I approach the throne of grace, we can do so with confidence, because Jesus has made a way for us to be reconciled to the presence of a Holy God."*

> Vertical Exhortation (leading the congregation in a prayer): *"Lord, we thank you that we can confidently approach the throne of grace. Because of your Son Jesus, we have audience with the you, Holy God."*

These exhortations essentially say the same thing; they're just directed differently. The difference is subtle, but it simply allowed Tori's youthfulness and gifting to coexist. In allowing this formative season, we set her up to succeed and we made it easier for the congregation to receive her ministry.

Youth Worship Ministry

Youth worship is not the B Team! Actually, the quality of our worship did not suffer when our youth worship team led the adult service. If you have a healthy vision for worship, you will attract musicians and many of these will be youth. Here is an axiom of musicians: "Good musicians like to play with other good musicians!" It becomes self-perpetuating. Especially in a community of believers who, because of Jesus, value the music *and* the musician. The attraction for good musicians is understandable. The learning potential is greater among good musicians.

Be intentional about giving your youth worship ministry every resource that is available to the adult worship ministry. You want to build the same vision (i.e., structure, accountability, expectations, value system) into the culture of the youth worship ministry. If this is neglected, there is a potential for the youth worship ministry to drift or seek a separate identity from the adult church (not the goal). Some of this is characteristic of youth, but we don't want, of neglect, to undermine the greater vision of promoting unity among the body— not to mention, the impartation of wisdom.

It's important to avoid separate song catalogs for youth and adult worship. You want your song catalog to be the same for both youth and adult worship. In addition to a common song catalog, we promoted unity by attending many of the youth services to encourage the youth worship leaders and teams. We also invited the youth worship leaders to attend a weekly general worship meeting and a monthly song meeting (discussed more in the Chapter 10). New song suggestions should meet the same scrutiny, evaluation, and standards regardless of whether it is a youth or adult worship song submission.

One interesting observation: many songs the youth submitted to this process found their way into our catalog of songs. Another innate characteristic of youth is they usually have a thorough and current appraisal of new songs. We did make a few exceptions for our youth catalog for songs that were obviously youth-oriented, and even some that piqued our curiosity enough to see how they were received. But the goal is always to preserve and maintain the vision of unity, and the final decision should remain with the worship pastor.

Here are some additional thoughts and ideas related to structure that have served as us well in executing our vision for worship.

Be Community-Minded

God dispenses many gifts, and nothing is intended to be wasted. If God has gifted someone to sing, play an instrument, or master the technical aspects of worship, it was granted with a purpose. My heart has always been to help creatives to discover the Father, find their gift, assist them in developing and finding context for their gift, and help them to deploy into their mission. It's very satisfying to see someone equipped, empowered, and released to fulfill their destiny.

In that spirit, we prefer to be community-minded when another church shares a need for personnel (or other resources). We celebrate when we are able to fill a need by releasing and blessing a musician or worship leader to another fellowship. This has happened many times and has proven only to expand our influence. We get regular calls from these sons and daughters who keep us apprised of their ministries, victories, and challenges. Consider the number of churches that are in need of musicians *who understand their role and gift*! What a blessing to the kingdom of God to share with another congregation a gifted worship leader, or a mature drummer, that could serve as a seed of gospel-centered worship in another community of believers.

Worship Small Groups, Fellowships & Retreats

An important and effective way of promoting community among your worship ministry is small groups, fellowships, and retreats. With the exception of the church staff, the worship team is likely to spend more time together in the course of a week (of necessity) than any other ministry of your church. It is a built-in community. But unfortunately, rehearsals alone are not ideal relationship-building opportunities. A rehearsal, like as not, will provide opportunity to test the limits of relationship rather than foster a relationship. We need opportunity to intentionally participate in one another's lives outside the context of music.

Considering the worship ministry is one of the most visible aspects of your church, it's worth the investment to support small groups, fellowships, and retreats specifically designed to encourage the worship ministry.

Worship Small Groups

Creatives are an odd bunch. So much so, they often have their own vocabulary! A conversation with musicians (who spend an inordinate amount of time staring at each other in a studio or rehearsal) can be quite confusing to an outsider, at the quantity and quality of the assumptions that are made on the English language.

Sometimes, for the sake of expediency, you might consider organizing a small group designed for creatives. Not the least of which would be a better use of schedules, to arrange the small group around rehearsals. We have done this in the past, and it has worked well. Ironically, many, who have no connection with the worship ministry, have opted to join the worship team small group. A small-group discussion in a room full of creatives can be very different, entertaining, and dynamic. Though I am irritated at people's insistence on bringing popcorn to every meeting. What's with that? (I'm kidding.)

Worship Retreats

I strongly recommend an annual worship retreat. This would ideally be a retreat center designed to accommodate your group in a pleasant, restful environment that promotes community. We have occasionally invited out-side speakers, but understand, the "download" (information) that is most valuable for your team is from your own worship leadership and should include a window of time for healthy discussion. By far, the two most valu-able elements of a good worship retreat are:

1. the opportunities for relationship building (e.g., one-on-one conversation, free time); and

2. the opportunity to worship together (the simpler the better).

Don't overschedule this retreat!

If the church can afford to pay for this retreat, it would be money well spent. When we consider the amount of time dedicated to practice, rehearsal, and preparation, and the investment in equipment that many of these team members spend, it's not an excessive gift to the worship ministry. And the church body will benefit immeasurably from the investment. But even if the church cannot afford to fund the retreat, it's still a beneficial and important annual activity.

Worship Fellowships

I recommend scheduling worship fellowships for many of the same reasons as retreats. Consider scheduling two or three each year. A Christmas party fellowship is a must. Just the elements of Christmas and creatives justifies selling tickets to the event. We had to stop the Ugliest Christmas Sweater Contest. Seems the term *ugly* was a relative term.

Other fellowship ideas: Fourth of July Fellowship and Cookout, Spring Worship Fellowship, and Fall Worship Fellowship.

A Shepherd's Thoughts

My father's choice of location for a garden I was to plow, plant, and maintain was a slight slope beside our barn. My first thought was, *Wouldn't level ground make better sense?* After all, I would likely be the one navigating the hill, which was beginning to look more like a mountain. I was convinced my father lacked the foresight necessary to plant gardens. Until it became necessary to *water* the garden. *Oh! Hey!* I thought. *How fortunate this water spigot is located on the uphill side of the garden. And each row of the garden receives water from this one source. I bet my dad didn't even think of that.*

This ideal structure of worship ministry may not seem relevant to your circumstances currently, but when you begin to see your worship and worship ministry through a gospel lens, you will have need of a sufficient structure and plan for growth. My confidence is not in my methods or experience, but in the transformational power of the gospel. When you turn on the "spigot of the gospel" in your ministry, the relevance and design of the structure will make better sense. We will be unpacking this reality in the chapters that follow.

CHAPTER 5

A Good Worship Leader Is a Shepherd First

I am grateful for the many people who have made deposits in me. And one of the obvious benefits is the opportunity to pay it forward. I have many I could list here as spiritual sons and daughters on these pages, who make and have made my life full. To invest in someone and watch them succeed beyond anything you could ever imagine is one of the most satisfying rewards in life. I am a very proud Papa.

My daughters Tana and Tori both are involved in their churches' worship ministries. Tori has shown a special anointing to lead not just songs, but to lead people into the presence of God (with understanding). She has absorbed everything I invested in her and is now operating at levels of understanding I did not coach.

One night as I was helping her prepare for a weekend worship set, I glanced at her laptop, which was open to this story she had written:

A HEALTHY POSTURE OF A GOOD WORSHIP LEADER

BY VICTORIA LYNN ELENBURG-CHAPMAN

Allow me to paint a word picture. A romantic restaurant with soft, pleasant music. The tables are lit by candles and warm hanging lights. The air is filled with a rose scent as the couple in the corner are completely transfixed on one another.

They hardly notice the waiter filling their water cups. The husband leans in and brushes his wife's hair away and whispers to her. Her cheeks blush, matching the roses around her, and she smiles in playful adoration of him. Their hands reach for one another and their rings shimmer in the candlelight. She leans in and whispers back as the waiter quietly sets their next course down in front of them. The couple's eyes gleam with joy as they release one another's hands and begin their meal, talking quietly.

They laugh once in a while, obviously enjoying one another's company. They commune together as if no one else is around, hardly even noticing the waiter who now quietly clears their plates. The husband is now speaking, a serious but kind tone in his voice.

The waiter begins to approach the table but hesitates and backs away, sensing the intimacy of the moment. The husband takes his bride's hands in his own and gently speaks to her. Her eyes begin to swim with tears, but her smile remains. They spend a moment in silent reverence. She squeezes his hand, and they both smile. He straightens and looks around as she retrieves a tissue from her bag. The couple lingers in the moment, then quietly exits.

The man is the bridegroom (Jesus).

The woman is the bride (the church).

The waiter is the worship leader.[2]

This story demonstrated Tori understood her role as a worship leader. I was proud of my daughter's profound understanding. It was one of those moments I realized, *She gets it!*

The best worship leaders, like the waiter, understand their role: to serve. Like the waiter in the scene, they resolve to go unnoticed. He is careful not

---

2 Victoria Lynn Elenburg-Chapman, "A Healthy Posture of a Good Worship Leader."

to interrupt their communion. And, heaven forbid, he distracts or flirts with the bride by drawing attention to himself! He carefully gauges the intimacy of the moment and uses his judgment of when best to approach. This is a healthy posture of a good worship leader.

Leading worship is a priestlike role; we set up "meeting places" for God's children to commune with Him. The priority is providing an environment for the congregation to have an encounter with God. A good worship leader realizes he is there primarily to serve this vision. Every detail of worship needs to be filtered through this priority (i.e., the team members, the song selection, the worship service flow). A good shepherd's primary concern is for the flock. One of my mentors, Kenny Thacker, said of this understanding: "We must learn we are not there to serve ourselves and our personal preferences, but the congregation's need."

Musical Competency

Musical competency is an obvious skill set a worship pastor or leader must possess. Musical competency is, of course, varied, but here are a few important considerations in evaluating a worship leader:

- Must be able to produce and arrange songs; thus, to effectively communicate and navigate musical concepts.

- A musically trained worship leader/pastor is more effective because they can converse on multiple levels with other musicians (trained and untrained).

- While it's not an absolute, it's best if they play an accompanying instrument. Apart from the advantage of having a better command of a song, it's a more effective way of communicating dynamic and direction to the team.

The Many Roles of a Worship Leader/Pastor

The worship leader/pastor role requires a serious crossroads of giftings when you consider all this person must manage. As an example, on Sunday morning alone, he/she needs the following:

- A sensitivity to the team (not just musicians, but technical personnel) to treat each one as a valued member of the team, whose hearts and lives need to be shepherded.

- To promote an environment that balances and values everyone's time by promoting respect of schedules and people in a way that preserves the stated values and vision of the worship ministry and the church.

- To maintain a proficiency level (musically and technically) that provides an environment for others to have a meaningful and undistracted encounter with God.

- To balance the priestly role of pastoring, leading, and teaching the meaning and value of worship both to the team and to the congregation.

- To lead songs with an awareness of the prompting of the Holy Spirit.

- To provide clear instruction and direction to the team and the congregation (simultaneously) during the song.

Did I mention all while watching over the flock, with the heart of a shepherd? Oh, and sing on pitch and don't miss any chords . . . that you have memorized!

I learned this concurrent awareness in the years of my concert artistry. The advantage a concert artist has is the familiarity of singing songs written many years prior; these were songs I had written and performed many times! I could actually perform the song on a subconscious level. This familiarity with the songs allowed a useful freedom. I was free to pray and talk with God about what to say, or perhaps what song to sing next. This became incredibly valuable to me as a worship leader—how to be in the moment, yet to be aware of God's steady voice. It's also why I encourage worship teams to know the song from the heart, as it provides great liberty and freedom to allow your heart to lean toward God in the moment. God quickens your heart to the eternal nature of the worship. There are simply more important things going on in the service than our music (or our performances). Consequential, eternal things.

A Learning Yearning

My first filter when looking for a good worship pastor or leader is humility. There is no limit to a leader's effectiveness if they take this learning posture: "I have something to learn from everyone!" If we adopt the attitude that all of God's creation is a *book of instruction*, why would we not take advantage of reading every page? We should learn to see everyone as a page in this magnificent book.

The quality I noticed about the most successful songwriters in Nashville was their habit of absorbing everything. Every songwriting session was an opportunity to incorporate new techniques of perhaps wrestling with a lyric or integrating a new chord pattern into their own style. Soon, the cumulative effect of this learning posture made for a well-rounded, excellent songwriter. But it requires humility to say, "I have much, still, to learn." A good worship pastor or leader has the humility to listen and the wisdom to extract useful knowledge.

Loves People

This, too, is often assumed, but should not be. A shepherd exists for the love and watch-care of the flock.

One of my favorite worship leaders is Bruce Menefee, a pastor at Gateway Church in Fort Worth, Texas (and one of my personal circle of counsel). We invited Bruce as a guest worship leader on many occasions. In my mentoring role to worship leaders, I would recommend they actively watch Bruce as he leads. Like the shepherd in my introduction, he is vigilant to watch over his flock. When Bruce leads, he is not consumed with himself or distracted by sheet music or a confidence screen; he is watching the flock from corner to corner of the room. His demeanor is one that communicates, "Are you getting this? Do you see the Father? I want you to enter into God's presence." His *shepherd's heart* is evident.

I attended a worship leader panel discussion in Nashville during Gospel Music Association week, where a question was posed to Jack Hayford (a well-known worship pastor and songwriter). Someone posed this question to him: "When you lead worship, do *you* worship?"

Jack thought about his answer and then replied, "Good question. Sometimes." I was impressed with his answer, because he was accepting the mantle of mentor/coach for young worship leaders that were listening to his counsel. In his answer, he removed a significant unrealistic weight of expectation: that responsible, authentic worship leadership should appear only as total abandonment to the worship.

Modeling worship is extremely important, but a worship leader must demonstrate situational awareness (in the room and in the Spirit). As an illustration, if I needed to go to Walmart, I would simply get in my car and go. Not much thought has to go into this task. But if I am leading a caravan of fifty cars, I need to be much more aware and intentional. I am leading, but is anyone following? I want to be sure everyone arrives at our destination. I sure would hate to lose someone. When making a turn at a red light, I need to give intentional direction and assure everyone made the turn and made the light. This awareness may seem like multitasking on steroids, but with time, it becomes subconscious.

When we lead others in worship, we can ill afford to abandon the congregation entirely by getting caught up in our own worship moment, any more than your soundman or visuals director can abandon their task in the moment. This being said, I will admit there have been times (as a worship leader) I have been overcome with God's goodness and have had no choice but to kneel or weep or step away from the microphone. But these are exceptions, not a common occurrence. I need to have sufficiently filled my cup in my preparations for leading, which will allow me to lead others to where I have already been.

When a congregation has sufficiently gathered their collective heart around a song, or a moment in worship, I often get the sense that all I did was kick a snowball down a hill. It needed only a shove.

A good worship leader models worship for his congregation, but because of his love for people, he will also exercise his watch-care over their participation in worship. It would be a mistake to assume that because you have a talented singer and musician, you have someone who has a heart for people. Avoid those who might use the stage of your church to merely showcase their talent. There is so much more at stake in the Spirit!

Takes an Active Role in Lives

Loving people requires an active role in their lives. Celebrate when they celebrate and mourn when they mourn. Get-well cards and phone calls are appreciated, but there's no substitute for having a friend sitting beside you at the loss of a loved one, at the birth of a child, or in life's chaotic moments. These time sacrifices build enormous amounts of relational equity and represent considerable investments in building the kingdom of God.

A shepherd will learn what God has put into the heart of those he leads and will invest in their calling. One of my first questions of a team member is "What has God put in your heart to do for the kingdom of God?" This does not always have to be about music. Alisha Speed was one of the most effective women worship leaders I've had the privilege of pastoring; nor did it hurt that she had a fantastic voice. She had a passion to help young women discover their own God-given identity and calling, which came easy to her since she had enormous influence with the women of our church. It was not a stretch to allow her this role with the women of our worship ministry.

A shepherd will invest in the spiritual maturity of those he leads. This is a gospel priority. Of course, we want spiritually mature team members (including tech), but not simply for the benefit of the worship ministry. We want mature, productive men and women for the kingdom of God—mature fathers and mothers, brothers and sisters, and youth. It is my conviction that worship ministry can be as effective as any other expression of the church in making men better fathers, husbands, and brothers; in making women better mothers, wives, and sisters. Every decision and directive of worship should serve the vision of investing in the maturity of our teams.

Sometimes love requires an honest discussion of realistic expectations (Proverbs 27:6). Most parents know the discussion that begins, "I must tell you something difficult to hear, but if I don't tell you, who will?" I know in my own experience as an artist and songwriter, these are the ones who will make *you* better. Leadership often requires that we sacrifice our own fear of rejection for the benefit of those we are called to lead. The truth is, these honest, heart-to-heart discussions yield great, surprising results.

One such surprise happened when I first started to pastor a worship ministry and was forced to have a frank discussion with a drummer I had inherited, whose sense of tempo wandered considerably (and he did not know how to play with a click (metronome). Considering drums are a foundational instrument, and our worship directive was to provide an *undistracted* environment, I knew I would need to address the conflict with him. He was a great team player and had a great attitude; because we value the *musician more than the music*, I wanted to honor his heart to serve by not questioning his character.

Ever the diplomat, I began by appealing to his sense of doing things with excellence. I said, "would you like to improve your craft?"

To which he replied without blinking an eye, "Not really. I'm very busy running my own business and really don't have the time to invest in getting better."

After a long pause, I realized this conversation was not going the way I had rehearsed it in my mind.

He continued, "I told the previous leader I'm not a very good drummer, but I will try to fill the need until you find someone better."

Still stunned, I asked, "So, you don't mind if I find a new drummer?"

"No, that's fine," he said. "It'll be a relief."

I don't think I had encountered a musician in my thirty years in Nashville who was as settled and centered in their own self-assessment as Steve was. His identity was not challenged by his ability to perform (or not perform). He was quite comfortable offering his gift to the extent it met a need.

To this day, this brother is a dear friend. I have used his story many times to communicate the importance of honest and realistic discussions.

There are those who may never be proficient enough to be on your platform, but this does not mark the end of your responsibility to that individual. The gospel confers value upon this person, so invest time to help them discover their true area of giftedness and help them to develop and deploy into this gifting.

Has a Balanced Understanding of Excellence

I have heard the term *excellence* used many times in describing goals for a worship ministry. "We need to do things with excellence," it is said. In Psalm 33:3, the psalmist tells us to worship *skillfully*. John Piper provides a clarifying definition of our pursuit of excellence:

> We will try to sing and play and pray and preach in such a way that people's attention will not be diverted from the substance, by

shoddy ministry nor by excessive finesse, elegance, or refinement. Natural, undistracting excellence will let the truth and beauty of God shine through.[3]

This immediately presents a challenge to good musicians. "What? Excessive finesse? I have aspired to these qualities my whole life. Now you say, 'Don't be so good that you distract people'?"

Take a breath. This balance can be accomplished in a way that honors God and the spirit of excellence.

The balance we seek on a Sunday morning is a clear, undistracted encounter with God. Where we clearly raise the standard of Jesus Christ as the object of our worship, through the filter of the gospel, in an aesthetically pleasing environment, for the glory of God!

Excellence is a relative term. Excellent to whom? Who, among us, is excellent? How would God define excellence? I would challenge a common use of this term in our vernacular to say that any definition of the word *excellent* that does not include "the value of people" is not the highest use of the term. God values people! I am not suggesting we abandon levels of proficiency or our directives, but many times, this term is used as an excuse to be exclusive. I have preferred people on my team who were not the better voices, but because I knew their testimony was powerful in the community. Their ministry to the community made them more effective in leading others to worship. These qualities must be esteemed in our process of defining *excellence.*

There are those who are immediately and obviously musically talented whom I have held at arm's length because they were exhibiting an unhealthy, orphan-type spirit by seeking a stage for performance, not a platform for ministry. This is why I prefer an "on-ramp" for embracing new musicians. Time and relationship ensure we are not exposing our congregations to

---

3 John Piper, "What Unites Us in Worship," Desiring God, October 1, 2003, https://www.desiringgod.org/articles/what-unites-us-in-worship.

unhealthy leaders. It also provides an opportunity to correct unhealthy beliefs regarding gifts, and greatly enhances a prospect's effectiveness when they are eventually invited to the platform (more on this in the discussion of on-ramps in Chapter 11). We are fulfilling our dual role to the team and the community by guarding our platform, and the congregation is much more willing to follow someone they are heart-deep in relationship with.

A Shepherd's Thoughts

A shepherd will use music to influence people for the gospel. A performer will use music to influence people to their performance and will tend to use only those who reflect well to this end. We want to be careful of entrusting leadership to those who exhibit this tendency and certainly those whose only qualifying value is their ability to sing and play an instrument (or, heaven forbid, simply look the part).

Consider these essential qualities of good worship leaders:

- Has a love for God

- Has a love for people

- Has a servant's heart

- Is a competent musician

- Has a balanced understanding of the term *excellence*

- Has the humility to learn

CHAPTER 6

The Matter of Worship and Performance

I had a friend in college who had dedicated much of her education and life to the pursuit of art appreciation. She studied art in the United States and abroad. Her eye for great art was certainly more refined than most, and she could stare at a Picasso for much longer than I cared to. My untrained eye is simply not attuned to the genius that is apparent to the world and discipline of painting. And, like painting, when you have dedicated time and love to God's creation of music, and have experienced its most powerful and noble applications, you learn to appreciate the difference between worship and performance.

The importance of the discussion of worship and performance is made necessary because we (worship leadership) often confuse and frustrate our congregations when we allow performance to distract from worship by not recognizing the subtle differences between the two. A primary role and responsibility for leading worship is to promote participation. I understand there is an innate, inextricable element of performance even in our worship, but excessive production and performance can have the effect of distracting a congregation from participating. In all honesty, sometimes it is so good, I just like to watch. The performances are world-class. Nothing wrong with that—praise God! It just doesn't fill the congregation's need of corporate worship. Or of promoting an environment for participation.

I am not opposed to music as performance any more than I would turn my nose upward at people consumed by their first glimpse of the ocean. God's creation is awesome to behold, even if the beholder does not acknowledge its Creator. Music, as with all of God's creation, is a great wonder! The difference becomes the degree to which one prefers to participate:

1. One can simply listen and marvel at the creation of music in a performance;

2. One can listen, marvel, and worship the Creator in a musical performance; or

3. One can participate, marvel, and acknowledge the Creator in worship.

The latter is the expectation of our congregations when they attend our worship services. They expect and have need to participate in the "performance" (so to speak) to fill their need of glorifying God (Psalm 29:1–2; I Corinthians 10:31; Ephesians 1:3–6; Philippians 2:9–11).

My nuanced position is that worship is the highest expression and purpose for the creation of music. Music was created for worship! And worship was created for God! It is simply the order of things.

A common example of this tension between worship and the need to perform is the worship leader who has a gift to ad-lib (to spontaneously improvise) the established and familiar melody. While it provides a nice platform for a demonstration of the leader's gift, it has the effect of confusing those who are trying (or needing) to follow. While it is artistically pleasing, and serves the need of the performer, it frustrates the congregation. We serve the congregation best by providing them with the most common and familiar melody so they can participate and worship.

Our overarching mandate as worship leaders is to glorify God and to serve others. Be mindful of speaking this clarifying vision and values often to your team. This, too, serves as a standard for musicians who often conflate their value as servants with a need to perform (which we discussed in the Chapter 1).

In the spirit of transparency, I will admit I still wrestle with performance, sometimes moment to moment. The temptation constantly presses upon me when I stand before an audience. But God, in His grace and mercy, has allowed me to experience the sweet benefits of cooperating with His design for music and worship. Nothing is quite so thoroughly convincing than to watch God moving over people with a remarkable and specific knowledge of the need of the moment that only God can know.

I can understand Paul's exhortation more: "I was with you in weakness, in fear, and in much trembling. And my speech and my preaching were not with persuasive words of human wisdom, but in demonstration of the Spirit and of power, that your faith should not be in the wisdom of men but in the power of God" I Corinthians 2:3–5 (NKJV).

The Subtle Temptation for Creatives

Music is God's creation, and we get to participate in presenting it to the world. God knows it is tempting to subconsciously entertain the idea that the audience is responding to us. After all, if I could somehow convince people that I had a hand in building Mount Everest, you might understand how tempting it would be to allow an audience to redirect its worship. This is the dilemma facing creatives. If we choose to be or are ignorant of the Creator, we are easily seduced into the lie that people are responding to us, which leads creatives into a cycle of disillusionment and discouragement.

The difference between worship and the need to perform has more to do with the heart motivation and spiritual posture before the Lord than an audible or visible posture. This subtle difference makes us vulnerable to the temptation to ignore it, or to resist the shame of admitting to a weakness. It's also the reason I wanted to devote a chapter in this book to it. The temptation to ignore this secret desire can be crippling, but an honest admission and discussion can bring liberation.

The beauty of the gospel in this matter is that it informs the willing heart of the superior nature of worship over performance. Maybe I am naive, but I don't believe I have ever pastored a musician who willfully made a choice for performance when confronted with the clarifying higher purpose of music—which is worship! I have seen this transformation firsthand. My role as a shepherd leader is to patiently invest the subtleties of the differences and the virtues of worship over performance.

Musical Transactions (Performance versus Worship)

When I first began writing songs, they were not very good (embarrassingly so). They were songs about funny characters, and songs about "love" . . . written with as much authority as a fifteen-year-old could have on the subject. From those early songs, I have made an interesting observation regarding the transactions that takes place between an audience and a performer (and the gospel maturation of that observation). When I sang my songs to my friends and family, I was giving them a song; in return, they were giving me approval and affirmation in the form of applause. This is a simple horizontal transaction.

Horizontal Transaction
(between a performer and an audience)

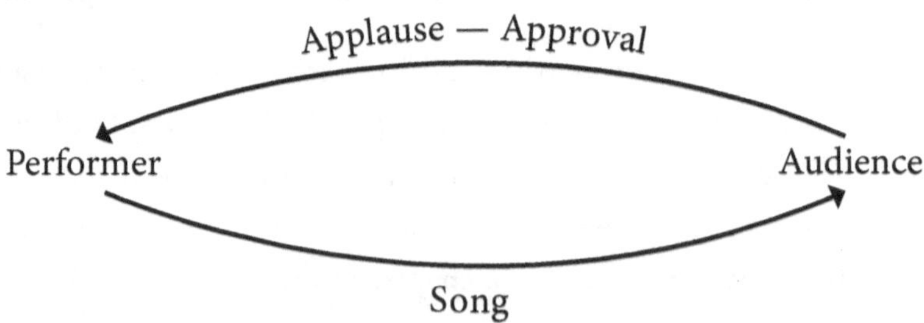

When I became a Christian, I began writing songs about my faith. My music took on another dimension; I gave the audience a song, they responded in much the same way as before, but I have introduced a redeeming value to my music by introducing my audience to Jesus. This added a vertical dimension to the transaction between me and my audience.

Vertical Transaction
(when a Faith dimension is introduced)

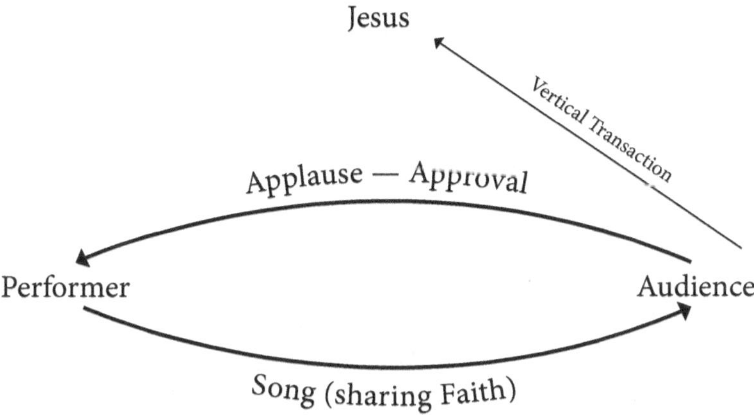

When I began to lead worship, I realized the full maturation of the transaction God intended for His creation. When we worship, the purpose and creation of music is perfectly fulfilled.

God gives us a song (the song of the redeemed); we (the worship team) present the song to the congregation to celebrate and have an encounter directly with God; God receives our praise and worship and responds to both the congregation and the worship team. First, to the worship team with affirmation and fulfillment for cooperating with His creation and design for music, and second, He responds to the congregation by inhabiting the praises of His people (see Psalm 22:3). This is both a vertical and horizontal transaction. In this manner, the creation of music is perfectly applied, God is honored and glorified, the congregation is blessed, and the musicians are fulfilled.

God's Intended Purpose
(for music and worship)

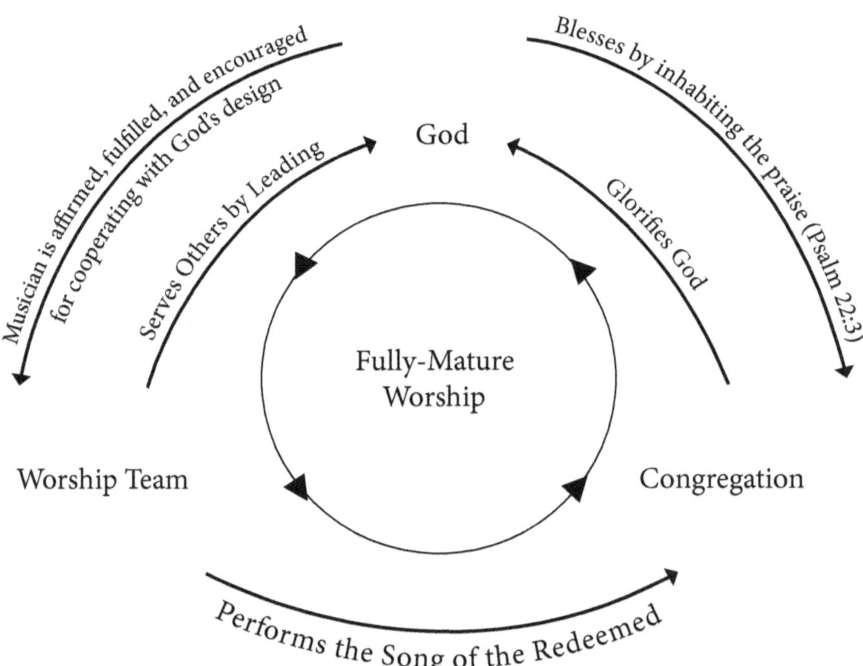

Those who struggle with a need to perform will resist this model (sometimes in subtle ways, and sometimes in obvious ways), as it removes the focus from the platform (performer) and toward the object of our worship (God). True worship removes the need for a horizontal transaction between a performer and an audience. True worshipers receive their affirmation and fulfillment from partnering with God in His creation of music. The performer, on the other hand, is still laboring under the perception that their affirmation comes from man (and his applause and approval). Here are a few examples of how this orphan spirit will reveal itself:

- It will insist upon melodies that divert from the established melody in order to feature their vocal versatility.

- It will insist upon being heard (turning up their instrument or amplifier) rather than contributing a complementary element of the presentation.

- It will insist upon songs that are not particularly congregational, but songs that appeal to individual preferences and tastes (See Chapters 9 and 10.)

- It will insist upon team members who only reflect well of a desired image.

- It will resent the promotion of others, as in a competition, rather than a team environment where we celebrate one another's accomplishments.

How do we avoid performing when music by its nature is inextricably woven into music?

Worship is the highest use of the creation of music; it is the genuine article. Worship is *why* we participate, performance is *how* we participate. We participate with God's design for His creation by *performing* music for God's glory (worship). As an illustration, federal agents don't learn to spot counterfeit money by studying the counterfeits. They study genuine bills until they master the look of the real thing. Then when they see counterfeit money, they recognize it. When we see worship through a gospel lens, we see the original design and performance becomes the lesser motivation.

A Shepherd's Thoughts

How does the gospel inform our response to this distinction between true worship and performance? My intent is to help you identify the offending spirit, not the offending individual. Be careful not to use these identifiers as a means of excluding people. Identifying weakness is not an opportunity for shame, but for growth. After all, I would likely be more successful at losing weight if I didn't have to depend upon food on a daily basis to subsist. And we would all be more successful in pure, undefiled worship if music did not require an element of performance. If we're honest, we all wrestle with these temptations from time to time. It's an extremely fine line to walk. But exposing unhealthy motivations serves to make us more effective and fulfilled in our gifts. Be patient—we all walk in ignorance until someone invests truth in love.

Worship is the higher purpose and use for God's creation of music! We, as creatives, are more fulfilled, more encouraged, and more affirmed when we participate with God's design for music and art: to worship Him.

CHAPTER 7

The Value of Singing the Gospel

George Frideric Handel was an eighteenth-century composer of operas.[4] One of the high points of his life and work was writing one of the most beautiful and magnificent works in the history of music: "Messiah."

Prior to writing his masterpiece, Handel had begun to develop health issues and his popularity was fading, which he believed marked the end of his career. In 1741, in despair and facing bankruptcy, he received an invitation to direct one of his works at a charity event in Ireland.

Instead of merely directing a previous work, he decided to write a new oratorio for the event. Being a religious man, he decided, unlike his previous works, to use Scripture as his text. In the writing of his new work, something supernatural began to happen. It is said his writing came with such a frenzy and urgency as unlike anything he had ever written before. People began to think perhaps he was under a spell or had lost his mind. His servants reported he seldom ate or slept and in the late night could barely grip his pen.

In fact, what Handel had discovered was God's design for His creation of music—the power of music combined with the gospel. In fewer than twenty-five days, Handel had written one of the world's greatest and most celebrated pieces of music – "Messiah". When he had finished, he sobbed, "I think that I did see all heaven before me, and the great God Himself!"

---

4 This story has been told and retold in many articles. Each is similar, but not verbatim. I have chosen to rewrite and abbreviate the story in my own words. In my research, I have discovered the original story is taken from *Spiritual Lives of the Great Composers* by Patrick Kavanaugh. Most of the accounts online are variations of the original.

When Handel chose to combine God's creation of music with the announcement of the gospel, he discovered music's most powerful and intended purpose: to glorify God.

Our world is thirsting, desperately, for the gospel. The gospel being the narrative of the life, the death, the burial, and the resurrection of Jesus Christ, and all of its implications in our lives. And yet, it is not uncommon in our current church culture to sit through an entire music service and never hear the name of Jesus in a song, in an exhortation, or in a transition. In our increasingly chaotic world, there is simply nothing more urgent or profitable than the propagation of the gospel.

Acts 4:12 (ESV) says, "And there is salvation in no one else, for there is no other name under heaven given among men by which we must be saved."

Avoid the temptation to compromise the content and message of the gospel for fear of irrelevance, or the fear of not being "woke." Choose and/ or write songs that embrace the gospel. Your congregation, confronted with the reality of a good song, may be entertained for the moment, but when confronted with the reality of the gospel, they will be changed for a lifetime. That which should separate the music of the church, from all other expressions of music, is the content and the message. The gospel (the reality of Jesus, and what He has accomplished for us) is the element that is most powerful. There is simply no other element more profitable in our corporate worship than to adequately raise the standard of Jesus Christ.

John Piper said:

> We do not avoid feelings of shame by altering the gospel to make it popular and inoffensive (see I Corinthians 1:18). We avoid feelings of shame by remembering that the gospel is going to be vindicated in the end. We remind ourselves that the gospel alone brings forgiven sinners to final, everlasting joy. Nothing in the world can do this except the gospel of Jesus Christ. Judaism, Buddhism, Hinduism,

Islam—they do not have a Savior who can solve the problem of separation from a Holy God through sin, and offer sinners hope by grace and not works. Only one message saves sinners and brings them safely into the presence of God: the gospel of Jesus Christ. It alone is the power of God unto salvation.[5]

Many Christian leaders are describing our current popular culture as a post-Christian culture, which is increasingly more accommodating of a universal concept of God and becoming more outrightly hostile toward Christianity. If we do not adequately raise the standard of Jesus Christ in our worship, we risk compounding the problem with powerless, meaningless, pointless, inauthentic, circular worship (worshipping the praise, and praising the worship), thus neglecting the object of our worship.

A helpful exercise is to reexamine our current song catalog through a gospel-centered filter. While a lyric that celebrates the literal gospel is extremely powerful, we are not limited to this alone. We can harness the power inherent in the gospel by reminding the worshiper of the *implications* of the gospel on every aspect of life. For example:

- If the worship song celebrates love, look for (or write) the lyric that describes how Jesus loves us.

- If the worship song celebrates hope, look for the aspects of the gospel that remind us how Jesus has made provision for hope. Jesus overcame death and the grave so you and I no longer have to fear death and the grave. What great hope leaps in the heart of the worshiper!

- If the worship song talks of mercy, look for the announcement that God showed His mercy toward us and gave His only Son that we might be reunited with Him.

---

5 John Piper, "The Gospel Is the Power of God unto Salvation," Desiring God, June 21, 1998, https://www.desiringgod.org/messages/the-gospel-is-the-power-of-god-unto-salvation.

Of recent, songs from some of the new worship writers have been encouraging. But I would stop short of calling it a renaissance. And, too, let's not dismiss the gospel-rich hymns of our church history! Let's not trade the wonder, simplicity, and majesty of the gospel for a watered-down, shallow counterfeit to accommodate the perception that the gospel is passé or ineffective.

Cultural Awareness

My son, the pilot, often uses a phrase "situational awareness," which is an acute grasp of everything going on around you. As pastors and leaders, we need to be keenly aware of cultural shifts and the specific needs within our community. One we most share in common is the subtle shift in consumeristic attitudes that have permeated the church. We shop our churches like shopping at Walmart, and we evaluate ministries within the church based on personal preferences.

Often when someone leaves a church, a version of this statement is heard: "I just wasn't getting much out of it." This is very revealing. We have retreated into a belief that church (and its music) exists to serve us rather than a place to discover God the Father, to develop our gifts, and to be deployed into our mission. When we get an accurate revelation of our role as church members, it will include an understanding of our role in that community. So, it's important to have an accurate definition of our role in community because it impacts our participation.

I've heard of a popular service that will print a special copy of a children's book with your child's name inserted as the main character in the story. The appeal is the story features your child, and the child is certainly more intrigued when they visualize themselves as a major participant in the story. I contend, "So do we adults!" We are naturally more interested when we see ourselves as part of the story. The gospel connects us to a grand narrative: God's story of redemption.

For example, the children of Israel learned their history through the stories told and retold from generations through songs they learned of how God rescued and redeemed them for Himself as God's chosen; also, they could see their direct ancestry in the stories and songs. We have wandered from this practice. We need to rekindle and reconnect with the grand narrative of God's story of redemption. If we recognized our role in partnering with God to build and establish His kingdom, we would not be so willing to participate in wholesale "gaps" in the narrative, or the omission of our ancestry: Jesus! We would insist the gospel be represented in our worship.

Why Is It Important to Sing the Gospel?

Apart from the value of hearing the gospel in the context of a beautiful melody and chord progression, here are other important reasons to embrace the gospel in our songs:

- Because God did. Zephaniah 3:17 (ESV) says God "will exult over you with loud singing."

- Because Jesus did. Matthew 26:30 (ESV) says in the upper room that Jesus and His disciples sang hymns together: "And when they had sung a hymn, they went out to the Mount of Olives."

- Because it promotes agreement and unity between the pulpit (the Word) and the music (the worship).

Why the emphasis on the gospel? Isn't God's creation of music powerful? Yes, but the music is not what unites us—it's the gospel. Get fifty people lined up to tell you what music genre will be used in heaven, you're likely to get fifty answers. It is the life of the One who created music that unites us.

Some years ago, I was asked to participate in a panel discussion at a worship conference. Many of the churches were having difficulty navigating the complexities of combining a traditional worship service and a contemporary worship service. As I shared then, they are both valid forms of worship. I have seen worship services that beautifully utilize both styles and that wonderfully complement the spirit of worship. Not only should contemporary and traditional be complimentary, but they should be combined regularly.

If you follow a wheat farmer long enough, you'll discover he's usually informed of the latest methods of producing the greatest yield for his annual crop. But his long-term love and care for his soil will include a healthy respect for the knowledge that has been passed down for generations. Why would we not use the best songs in the history of the church—the hymns? Why would we not use current worship songs (some of which are awesome)? Why can we not use all gospel-centered songs to produce the greatest yield? Why can't old and new coexist to help us connect our worship to *the* grand story of our redemption?

Many times, I have used the chorus of the hymn "How Great Thou Art" as a tag at the end of the contemporary song "How Great Is Our God" (Tomlin/Reeves/Cash). This effect unites the generations in worship. God is all over this! Get creative with the old and new, and let God work.

The danger of separating the services (according to musical style) is the unintended consequence of promoting two separate congregations, which usually falls to young and old. Ask one difficult, all-important question that might impact both the worship and the pulpit: "Is the gospel being adequately esteemed in our church culture?" The gospel should inform every expression of your church life. The benefits of a unified, multigenerational church body far exceed any perceived benefit of catering to a musical style.

In Ephesians 2:14 (ESV), Paul says, "For he himself [Jesus] is our peace, who has made us both one [Jew and Gentile] and has broken down in his flesh the dividing wall of hostility."

Jesus not only abolished the wall between Jew and Gentile, but he leveled the wall between generations, between nationalities, between race, class, and (God help us) traditional and contemporary. The gospel elevates us above this type of thinking.

It's not the music that unites us—it is the gospel.

Objective and Subjective Worship

When establishing a vision for worship (revisit Chapter 3), it's important to distinguish between objective worship and subjective worship.

Objective worship is nonnegotiable, as this is the content of the songs. The songs must be theologically sound: God-focused, God-exalting, and gospel-centered. The content of our worship is nonnegotiable.

Subjective worship, on the other hand, is negotiable, which is the style of music (genre). Sometimes these factors are dictated by our resources (people, gifting, etc.). Celebrate the musicians God brings, even if they're not as proficient as you would hope. If your community is full of accordion players, well . . . you are a pioneer in probing the outer limits of God's grace. But seriously, make the best of it! If your fellowship is full of country musicians, then work on being a great gospel-centered country worship team. The style of music is negotiable. The gospel compels us to love and invest in the musicians God brings us.

My favorite Far Side cartoon is Saint Peter standing at the gates of heaven saying, "Welcome to heaven, here's your harp." The next frame shows the devil standing at the gates of hell saying, "Welcome to hell, here's your accordion."

What style of music will be preferred in heaven? I don't know, but I do know it will be focused on the Lamb of God: Jesus! (See Revelation 5.)

The Value of Liturgy

A liturgical service can be a gospel-rich environment. Liturgical worship is typically more scripted and more scripturally rich, with an emphasis on the sacraments and responsive reading and can be quite liberating and valuable to experience worship without all the trappings of music. How many times do we sit in a service and evaluate the quality of the worship service solely for the music? The music should not distract from the content (the gospel).

Many of the well-known hymns were written by John and Charles Wesley. It's useful to know that in their day, they were writing for a people who were largely illiterate. Writing a doctrine-heavy lyric was intended so their congregation could learn and retain the doctrine. This is an example of an "acute awareness" of your community; knowing they would more easily remember a song taken from a popular (bar room) melody, they packed them full of doctrine-rich lyrics. But to the point, the music served as the vehicle to impart doctrine.

Music is a vehicle, but it's most powerful when used for its created purpose: to promote the gospel. For those congregations that have been immersed in the extreme (lots of emotion, lots of energy and performance), liturgy could be expanding.

A Shepherd's Thoughts

When my children were young, they would have preferred a Happy Meal from McDonald's at most every meal. But thankfully my wife Cindy knew their need for proper nourishment would require more thought than Ronald McDonald was offering. The temptation, for us as worship leaders, is to cater to consumer-driven perceptions of worship, which are too often focused on emotions and performance. I confess, it *is* more fun to lead an enthusiastic, responsive congregation. But shepherding our congregations in worship is a sobering responsibility. God places great responsibility on those called to lead and care for his people.

Hebrews 13:17 (ESV) says, "Obey your leaders and submit to them, for they are keeping watch over your souls, as those who will have to give an account."

Avoid the trappings of evaluating your success by the number of raised hands, or the number of those engaged. An engaged enthusiastic congregation is good as long as they're responding to exalted thoughts about God (the gospel) and passionate affections for God (a grateful response to the gospel), not a contrived emotional response to a dynamic production or performance.

The distinction between the music and the content is important. We can easily miss the unifying element of our worship, which is the gospel. Music (apart from the gospel) can become divisive, if we are unaware of this subtle distinction. By all indications, God intended music and the gospel to be complementary. (Read Revelation 5.)

As a shepherd, keep a watchful eye over your congregation's needs and ensure your worship is filling that need. Recognize when small course corrections would be a benefit to your congregation (even if only for a season). Seek a balance that engages the hearts and the minds of your congregation.

CHAPTER 8

Elements of a Gospel-Centered Worship Service

Planning an effective gospel-centered worship service is an important element of worship ministry. There is little teaching on this, but when it's done well, it's noticeably powerful. Gospel counsel informs us that relationships and quality time are the foundations for this element and the best nuggets require deeper *mining*. Let me explain.

In the mid-nineties, I received an unusual invitation to a beautiful, isolated cabin in the Smoky Mountains in North Carolina; not to do a concert, but to just sing a few songs and lead worship for four pastors over five days. These four pastors were college and seminary buddies who had established this annual retreat to remain intentional and faithful to their life-giving relationships with each other.

I was quite envious of their genuine love and care for one another, as they shared details of each other's families and discussed challenges they were navigating in their own lives and fellowships. But this annual retreat was also a work retreat. They asked and listened to each other regarding direction for their messages over the next year. They asked, "What are you hearing God say? Is this unique to your congregation? Is this unique to your community? What do you sense God is saying to the church?"

I could not help but be impressed at the care and thought these pastors were investing in the messages they were preparing for their congregations. I wondered if their fellowships knew and appreciated how well they were being pastored, and how much thought was going into their watch-care.

As worship leaders and worship pastors, we should prepare with no less soberness of task. While these types of retreats are common among lead pastors, they are not so common among worship pastors and leaders. As with my pastor friends in North Carolina, we need these times to:

1. think big picture;

2. plan long term;

3. evaluate the state of our worship ministries (songs and teams);

4. encourage and be encouraged;

5. compare challenges and solutions; and

6. invest in God's kingdom outside of your own community.

In general, time to allow God to *fill your leadership cup*! Love God, love your congregations, and love yourself enough to care for your own soul; regularly get away with edifying relationships for the purpose of hearing God in a community of other worship leaders and pastors. Conferences are good, but a small retreat like these pastors honored annually is a different *download* and will refresh your soul.

Another foundational and critical element for planning the roughly fifty-two church services each year is the relationship between the lead pastor and the worship pastor. This needs to be an intentional relationship with weekly quality time to talk and pray together. Let's face it: the weekly Sunday morning service is the broadest touchpoint with our congregations and communities, and the worship is easily 40 to 50 percent of that touchpoint. Our Sunday service is a small one- or two-hour window that should be prayerfully and strategically planned—if not exclusively, at least including the two individuals who will occupy most of the face time.

Where to Start with These Foundations

Begin your preparation for a worship service with a good feel for the message. Not just the text. Many messages can be extracted from a text, so ask specifically of the pastor, "What is your message for the congregation?" Choose songs that will support the message (or the series of messages). This is always a good test of your song pool, where we learn that gospel-centered songs (like the gospel itself) are deep and wide and cover a vast ground of application, when needed.

On one such occasion, I asked Pastor David, "What will your message be this week?" To which he replied, "When Jesus cast the demons out of the two men into the herd of pigs that threw themselves over a cliff into a lake and drowned."

His blank face provided me no further clarity.

After a pregnant pause, I said, "Okay . . . several songs spring to mind." My response revealed my purpose for asking, and we had a good belly laugh!

It's not always possible for the worship to perfectly complement every message. That's okay. This is where your investment in the foundations of quality time and strategic relationships will manifest. In these instances, choose songs that serve the greater needs of the congregation and the church. God can, and often does, spontaneously inhabit these moments with remarkable specificity.

Templates for a Worship Set

This is by no means an exhaustive list, but it is helpful in seeing and learning how to develop and create different themes for a worship set:

- Celebrate the Trinity:

    - A song about the Father: "How Deep the Father's Love for Us" by Townend.

    - A song about the Son: "Jesus Messiah" by Carson, Tomlin, Cash, Reeves.

    - A song about the Holy Spirit: "Holy Spirit" by Torwalt or the hymn "Spirit of the Living God" by Iverson.

- Educate your congregation on the value and protocols of the tabernacle:

    - Songs that represent the gates of thanksgiving, the outer courts of praise, the inner courts of worship, and the intimacy of the holy of holies.

    - Though Jesus removed these dividing walls into God's presence, the tabernacle provides a visual illustration of how God prefers to be approached. *How to Worship a King* by Zach Neese provides a deep dive into this discussion. It's a great read and study for you and your worship ministry.

- Matt Boswell suggests these principle elements be represented in a good worship service: God – Man - Christ – Response

    - A song about the descriptive nature of God: "Your Great Name We Praise" by Kauflin.

    - A song about the descriptive nature of man, or man's hopelessness apart from God (i.e., sin, our need of a savior): "Amazing Grace (My Chains Are Gone)" by Walker, Pritchard-Blunt, Tomlin, Giglio.

- o A song about the solution/the cross, death, burial, and resurrection: "Jesus Paid It All" by Hall.

- o A song of response to all we have sung: "Goodness of God" by Ingram.

- At Easter, consider songs that flow in the order of events as they happened, such as the Last Supper, the Cross, Jesus's death, or His burial, then end with a song about the Resurrection of Christ!

These are just a few creative ways of planning a thoughtful gospel-centered worship service.

Visualize taking your congregation on a journey. For example: We enter His gates with thanksgiving (Psalm 100:4). The outer court is where we celebrate and exalt God and all He has done. Then as we move into the inner court, we begin to prepare our hearts for the holy of holies and we become more introspective with songs that contemplate the holiness of God. Then as we enter the holy of holies, we need songs that foster intimacy between the bride and the bridegroom. And, even when we are leaving the holy of holies, do so with a sensitivity that shows a respect for where your congregation has just been.

We've all been in a service when the announcements (following a holy moment) are handled with the sensitivity of a bull in a china shop. If you've done well leading your people to a sweet and holy place, the last thing you want to do is immediately interrupt their sanctuary with an announcement: "Reminder . . . uh . . . we still need diapers for the children's ministry!"

As a child, after a good nap, I always appreciated my mom's tone at my bedside rather than my father's. My mom might lure me from my slumber with a snack; my father, on the other hand, pulled the covers from my feet and twisted my big toe until I had no choice but to roll out of bed. What a rude awakening! Exaggerated to make a point, but write and choose songs that shepherd your people in and out of the presence of God, with a sensitivity of the eternal nature of the moment. Allow them to experience each of the unique dynamics of approaching (and leaving) God's holy of holies, with songs that facilitate these different and unique dynamics.

In general, guard the Sunday service with a zealousness for what is most important to the life of the church. Plan elements, such as announcements and offerings, with as little interruption to the service flow as possible, and with a sensitivity to the congregation.

Calls to worship, exhortations, and transitions all serve to assist in leading your congregation on this worship journey. They announce where we are in our journey and instruct where we are going. Let's unpack each of these elements, as they are vital in serving the spirit of planning a gospel-centered worship service.

Call to Worship

In the chapters of this book, I've been promoting the value of *flow* in worship. I understand there are many necessities and demands placed upon the Sunday morning service, but a clear call to worship is very important. Alan Wright (author, pastor, and speaker) provides this description of the call to worship:

> The Call to Worship is an invitation to make a transition from the mundane to the transcendent. Calling people to worship is inviting them to become aware of God's presence. The Call to Worship is like a mother waking up her child in the morning – it shouldn't startle, but it shouldn't leave the child asleep. Our Call to Worship announces to those who have ears to hear: Awaken to the reality of God in your midst! "Lift up your heads, O gates! And be lifted up, O ancient doors, that the King of glory may come in" (Psalm 24:7 ESV). As King David called upon the doors of the tabernacle to make way for the glory-soaked ark, we call upon hearts to open wide – make space for the glory of God.[6]

6 Alan Wright, Theological Roundtable 2018, Gospel Proclamation, Worship Kerygma Ministries, pg. 26. Permission granted.

A call to worship requires creative thought. How do we engage a husband and wife whose words to each other on the way to church were not particularly edifying? Or a mother and father whose child may have quite literally thrown up on them on the way to church? How do we prepare them for the contrast they are about to experience? We hope to lead them into a reality that makes their worldly concerns seem small in comparison to the grandeur and majesty of the presence of God. A good worship leader will prepare his call to worship and transitions with the same care and thought as the pastor has for his message to the congregation. For example:

> Many of you have made a sacrifice of time, money, and energy to be here this morning, especially parents of young children. Isaiah 55:1 (ESV) says, "Come, everyone who thirsts, come to the waters; and he who has no money, come, buy and eat! Come, buy wine and milk without money and without price." While the living water God offers is without price, and while it is offered to us at no cost, it came at great cost to Him. Let's celebrate and receive what God sacrificed, and what Christ suffered on the cross, and all it has purchased on our behalf.

Another example:

> Welcome this morning! I'm going to share with you from Philippians 2:9–11 (ESV): "Therefore God has highly exalted him and bestowed on him the name that is above every name, so that at the name of Jesus every knee should bow, in heaven and on earth and under the earth, and every tongue confess that Jesus Christ is Lord, to the glory of God the Father."

This scripture passage is enough, but if God gives you an insight to the Word, take your liberties and share your insight.

The priority for a call to worship is to prepare your congregation for ultimate reality: the *spiritual* reality. Paul provides an illustration to those at Corinth in I Corinthians 13:12 (ESV): "For now we see in a mirror dimly, but then face to face. Now I know in part; then I shall know fully, even as I have been fully known."

Transitions/Exhortations

As I have shared, visualize the service and the transitions and move the congregation through the planned worship service structure. Some worship teams have been playing together for many years and have achieved "spiritual sync." They don't require much musical preparation or discussion for transitions. But, if you're like most of us, we are working with different musicians every week, and we need to plan, talk through, and practice transitions. The instrumentalists can take ten minutes at the end of a Sunday morning run-through and practice these transitions by ending song A and transitioning to song B. It's not complex or time-consuming.

But for the worship leader, it requires more time and thought. It might take the form of an exhortation, a prayer, or a scripture reading. An exhortation in this context is usually an encouragement or prompting of the Holy Spirit intended to edify the congregation; but it also provides a bridge from song A to song B. This can be a musical bridge or a prayer that moves us from the outer court to the inner court.

Even a well-planned transition can go awry with a simple misplaced word. David Baroni, a dear friend, artist, songwriter, and worship leader, told me how he scrambled his words during a rather serious transition in the service by exhorting the congregation to "come . . . worship *us* together with the Lord!" David said it did not have the same impact as what he intended to say, which was to "come . . . worship *the Lord* together with us!" I would be tempted to return to the front gate and start over.

While I promote careful planning and prayer to transitions, it should not be assumed that I am against the spontaneity of spirit-led worship. Ideally, this is the goal or standard we are striving for. But until the worship leader and the worship team can effectively navigate a spontaneous level of transitioning, these fundamental steps will provide a training regiment. Exercise patience in waiting for this maturity to develop. The worship leader must not outpace his team, even if he has the ability to do so. Pastoring and shepherding a worship team is not a *sprint*. It is a *marathon*. Patience is an important element of building a safe and creative culture for your team. You go and grow together as a team!

Before we leave the topic of calls to worship and transitions, I would like to add two overarching thoughts. First, unless the lead pastor has given you (the worship leader) the authority otherwise, keep your transitions brief and on point. Worship fills a unique and separate need in our souls from the spoken word. Let it be a sober exception when you interrupt your congregation's worship focus. Remember, if we are planning our worship journey well, we want to lead well. Let the transitions serve the journey and provide direction to the congregation.

Second, and not to sound contradictory, it's fine to let the congregation see you think. I always appreciate when someone respects my time and attention enough to consider well what they are wanting to communicate. I am not suggesting long pauses (like unpreparedness), but in a way that communicates a measured exhortation. I would rather someone slow down and speak to the congregation in the moment than to listen to someone recite a series of words they have memorized (and may or may not understand themselves).

This is a personal preference, but in this way, I gravitate toward contemplative worship leaders. I know it's not the popular personality type we see in this role, but I think the long-term impact of a thoughtful, quiet, introspective, attentive musician makes for a great worship leader. Here's how that translates on the platform: he doesn't care to speak, but when he does, it usually carries a significant weight in the spirit. Everyone leans in to this worship leader's transitions and calls to worship.

The Value of Silence

As a musician, it might surprise you to know that I think one of the most valuable dynamics of worship can be silence. Yes, silence. I wonder if anyone has written that song? "I'd like to introduce a new song I just wrote called 'Silence.'" It might be more popular than you'd think!

Legendary Nashville drummer Kenny Malone said of his creative process and approach to playing drums on a song: "Is what I'm preparing to play better than silence?" This demonstrated a healthy appreciation for what served the song best (big-picture awareness), and this kind of awareness separated him from the many other session drummers. Oh, that we would approach our planning of a worship service with the same foundational respect of silence.

We don't value silence the way God does. Some of the most precious moments I have ever experienced are the times I managed to be still and silent and to <u>listen</u> to what God wanted to say to me. In these moments, His words are typically few but amazingly profound—words that speak to corners of my heart that I wasn't even aware existed.

I wrote a song of this experience called "To Hear My Father's Voice":

I do not take for granted where I stand is holy ground
I would not desecrate this blessed refuge that I've found
I would tell you Lord how excellent is Your name above all names
I could tell how much You mean to me, for Your worthy of all praise
But when my spirit is empty, and words of life are all too few
More than a prayer of adoration Lord, I need to hear from You
I Need to Hear My Father's Voice
There's calm assurance in the quietness,
Like fresh anointing oil
I Need to Hear My Father's Voice
To be a blessing, I must first be blessed
Before I walk, I need that place of rest
Lord spill Your cup of holiness on me[7]

We don't do silence, solitude, or quietness very well in our current culture. Yet these are essential in communing with God. God's Word becomes more

---

7 "To Hear My Father's Voice," Tony Elenburg / Tana Kaye Music (ASCAP) © 1992.

clear when I am not distracted. His comforting words become more relevant when I pray in solitude. Learn to lead your people to these still waters.

A good shepherd will always choose grazing for his sheep near streams of running water. But not fast running streams. Sheep are prone to drowning in fast moving water because their wool absorbs moisture quickly; thus, the good shepherd will lead them to still waters. How appropriate then are the words concerning the divine Shepherd: "He leadeth me beside the still waters" (Psalm 23:2, KJV).

Don't be afraid to lead your congregation to silence. It will seem to some as the most awkward moment of the service, but when it's spirit-led, it will be remarkably powerful. Sometimes you will hear whispers of prayers or holy and sweet sobbing, but don't rush. Teach your congregations the value of what it means to be still, and know that He is God (Psalm 46:10; paraphrased). To be confronted in these moments with the reality of who God is (and how much He loves us) would be the answer to every question of man, the moment of resolution for mankind, and certainly, the high point of any worship service.

Many times, it is the spontaneous, unplanned silent moments of a worship service that are most meaningful. Learn to rest in the moments when God is *moving over* the congregation; pray over them, in this manner (to yourself): "Lord, pour yourself over them as anointing oil. According to the need of every person, let yourself be known. Let them know you care deeply and intimately for the details of their lives."

Practice moments of stillness and silence with your congregation. This also provides them an opportunity to see the clearest reflection of their own heart. After this service, you can expect many different responses from people, but know this: The level of awkwardness one experiences with silence is in direct proportion to their need for it!

A Shepherd's Thoughts

Planning a good gospel-centered worship service requires more planning, thought, and prayer than most people would realize. The most demanding each year are the Easter and Christmas services. Few people, apart from the worship pastor and/or leader, have an appreciation for the hours and details that go into these presentations. These major services come and go in a matter of days, and still there are fifty other services of equal importance to plan and prepare.

These other fifty services are where the relational deposits (with the lead pastor and other leaders) will pay off. The withdrawals from this relational equity are more from the spirit you share in common than the verbal exchanges needed when planning your services. The foundational vision, mission, and values are understood.

When I travel, I like the wide-open roads that allow me to use my cruise control. It allows me to focus on other things. I'm free from the burden of watching my speed constantly. When planning meaningful weekly gospel-centered worship services, we need the freedom and time to focus on the important things. This allows us to focus on the finer points of the service, like calls to worship and transitions.

I like to pray during the week and ask God to give me a vision for the finer points of the service. What should I share? What scripture would be good to open the service with? How should the announcements be handled following the intimate worship this week? What closing song will best serve the message the pastor is sharing this week?

In your planning, let the heart of Jesus (the gospel) and His love for people inform every decision you make.

CHAPTER 9

Evaluating Songs for Worship

Of the many responsibilities of worship pastors and leaders is the importance of choosing songs for our congregations. In this chapter, I would like to dig a little deeper on the worship element of the song and draw attention to the value of gospel-rich songs.

A good place to start in formulating your evaluation process is a comprehensive and honest appraisal of your song catalog and your congregation. Consider this exercise with the help of your pastors and elders, and ask each their opinion of the general state of your worship:

- Would you define our worship songs as gospel-rich? Do our songs celebrate Jesus and all that He has done for us?

- Are we heavy on songs of response (defined as songs that express how we feel about what God has done for us)?

- Do our songs promote agreement between the worship and the Word? Do our songs reinforce the messages from our pulpit?

- What would you consider to be the unique spiritual needs of our church and community?

With this information, consider the songs you've asked your congregation to sing in the past month. The ideal result would be, of course, a gospel-rich worship environment where we esteem and celebrate who Jesus is and all He has done for us, with a proportionate number of songs of response. Should your evaluation reveal an imbalance (i.e., an inordinate number of songs of response), consider adjusting your catalog accordingly by looking intentionally for more gospel-centered songs in spite of perceived notions of song popularity.

Here are a couple of examples I've heard from an evaluation of songs for gospel content:

- "My congregation is passionate about worship! From the first note, they're all-in. But our songs are gospel-deficient. Our songs are long on expressions of our love for Jesus, and expressions of what we long to do for Him, but they are short on describing what Jesus has done for us."

  - Remedy: Find more songs that declare His nature, His attributes, and His actions toward us.

    - Recommendations: "His Mercy Is More" by Matt Boswell and Matt PaPa; "In Christ Alone" by Keith and Kristyn Getty.

- "Our congregation is very reserved. We see very few visible expressions of worship in our service. Our songs are theologically sound and gospel-rich, but we would like to see more people engage their hearts in passionate worship."

  - Remedy: Don't neglect the benefit of educating your congregation on gospel-centered worship, but you might need more songs of response that allow the congregation to express their passion for Jesus and a thankfulness for all He has done on our behalf.

    - Recommendations: "Good Good Father" by Anthony Brown and Pat Barrett; "Graves into Gardens" by Brandon Lake, Christopher Joel Brown, Steven Furtick, and Tiffany Hammer.

Balance

I understand it's difficult to choose songs when there are so many filters and considerations of pace, flow, theological soundness, congregational needs, familiarity, freshness, etc. But the process becomes more manageable when you have a healthy and balanced catalog of songs to choose from.

Many of the current songs are what I would categorize as songs of response, which are fine and needful. But seek balance in your song catalog by adding songs that are focused on the attributes of God, or the nature of God, and what He has done for us. Consider songs that unite the congregation with words like *we* or *us*. These promote a spirit of unity around the object of our worship: Jesus!

Note: A key sequence to consider is, songs of response are most effective after the object and standard of our worship has been adequately identified. When a clear standard of Jesus Christ has been raised in worship, then a song of response is well positioned and effective.

A suggestion after your evaluation of current songs: consider categorizing them according to their intended purpose:

1. Songs of Praise:

    a. Songs that declare who God is (his nature and attributes).
    b. Songs that celebrate what He has done (His actions toward us).

2. Songs of Worship:

    a. Songs that promote an encounter with God.
    b. Songs that promote intimacy, surrender, relationship, and dedication.

3. Songs of Response:

    a. Songs of confession, thanksgiving, gratitude, and adoration.

4. Songs of Invitation:

    a. Communion, confession, supplication, petition, and prayer.

A Practical List of Filters for Evaluating Songs

To help evaluate songs, put together a team made up of musicians, worship leaders, pastors, and/or elders (in general, those who carry a burden for worship). The more diverse the group, the better. You will learn to appreciate the varied perspectives.

After my tenure at Lighthouse, Jeff Hook became our worship pastor. I love Jeff's passion for worship and was honored to serve with him. Jeff conducted a great monthly "new song" meeting. He regularly sent reminders to a short list of people (who carried our heart for worship) to submit song suggestions for the monthly meeting. He was always prepared with audio recordings and lyric sheets to help make our evaluations.

As we became more informed as a team of the filters we had established, we were all much more aware and sensitive to songs that did not meet the standard. As a result, in time, it became harder for songs to pass our filters and standards. It was satisfying, and somewhat humorous, to catch the glances and nods from other team members while listening when we began to collectively recognize an obvious shortcoming of a potential new song. Here are some questions you can consider with your team:

1. Is the song theologically sound?

There's a lot going on when we present songs to our congregation:

- We are giving them a song they can use to have an encounter with God;

- We are promoting agreement and unity; and

- We are facilitating communion with God.

We certainly want to make sure the song is theologically sound. If you find that an explanation is required to understand a lyric, or a need to convince the congregation of its value, then put simply, the author has failed to deliver the song. Unfortunately, when the song is excellent, except for one word or phrase, it's tempting to change a lyric, but this is not appropriate, unless you have permission from the author or publisher to do so. (Note: I have exercised this option a few times and have received permission to change the lyric, with provisions, so don't be discouraged from asking.)

2. Is the song congregational?

This is a finer point of writing worship. Some writers seem to have a better grasp of this subtlety than others. As much as we musicians get bored of simple melodies, our congregations are not participating for the entertainment or melodic value, but as a means of communing corporately with God. Be mindful of the priorities of giving the congregation a song they can sing and call their own, lyrics they can digest and identify with, and melodies they can easily sing and remember.

Congregational elements to evaluate:

- Is the song melodically complex? Are there complex intervals such as octaves? Are the melodies repetitive enough to promote participation?

- Is the song rhythmically complex? Are there multiple triplets? Or run-on triplets (if so, you will lose the one)?

3. Is this a well-crafted song?

Good songs begin with a good idea. "Jesus Paid It All" is a sweeping, profound statement; it covers a lot of the implications of the cross. Well-crafted verses will point to the profound statement again and again:

And when before the throne, I stand in Him complete

Jesus died, my soul to save, my lips shall still repeat

Chorus: Jesus paid it all . . .

A well-crafted song will leave your congregation with a clearly articulated thought, such as "Amazing Grace." The verses exist and celebrate the central theme of God's grace:

Through many dangers, toils, and snares

I have already come.

'Tis Grace hath brought me safe thus far

And Grace will lead me home.

All considered, determine to establish high standards for your song catalog. Many songs may pass your craft standards and your theological standards, but still may not appeal to you or the spirit of the house (the general vision and mission of the church). In that spirit, here are other acceptable responses in evaluating songs:

- "I don't care for the song."

- "I don't think this song meets the standard we have set for our song catalog."

- "I think there are better songs available to us."

- "I like the song, but our congregation is not that hip. They clap on the one and the three!"

A Shepherd's Thoughts

I understand how fun it is to do a new song with an enthusiastic congregation. Especially if it checks off all our boxes and expectations of a gospel-centered song. But our priority as worship pastors and leaders has to be the shepherding of hearts in worship. This requires a thorough appraisal and understanding of the needs of your congregation and a willingness to do what is best for their souls *first*.

I would recommend you pray for wisdom regarding the needs of your congregation, determine what adjustments you may need to make in your song catalog, review (and memorize) your standards for song evaluations, and pass every song through your new priorities and filters. You will gradually begin to see the power of the gospel transform your worship from just music to powerful ministry. It works!

CHAPTER 10

Writing Songs for Worship

In my concert/artist career, I would occasionally find myself scheduled to provide music for conferences (special music and/or worship). These conferences afforded me opportunities to hear very good teachers and preachers (some very well-known). I would take advantage of my good fortune and participate in as many sessions as possible. I would take notes and absorb all I could. The truth is, many of my songs were birthed from the ideas I gathered in these conference sessions.

At one particular conference, my hotel room was next door to the main speaker. We shared a few meals together in the hotel restaurant. I had been blessed by his nightly messages to the conference and was excited to have his undivided attention at our meals together. I listened mostly, as was fortunate, because he talked mostly.

Among many subjects was a discussion of music; he shared his thoughts on the new worship movement (somewhat new at that time). Though he was complimentary and encouraging of my music and leadership at the conference, he was especially concerned and interested in talking about the new worship songs that were being written and sung in many churches.

I did not feel a need to defend the new worship music, but I listened intently, as I was integrating more worship music into my concerts. My concerts were typically just me, my guitar, and a stool. It's difficult to hold long the attention of an audience with just a guitar! I discovered worship songs made for very useful transitions—a break from listening intently, to participating in a song, which in turn prepared the audience to listen again.

Worship songs were merely elements of "pace" in my concerts. I admit this demonstrated a limited understanding of worship at the time.

But over several meals, he was providing me a broad historical perspective of music in the church and the varied qualities of the hymns—qualities that, in his words, were "lacking" in the new worship music. My first thought was, "Here we go again. Old people who associate their passions and faith with old songs!" But the more I listened, the more I learned.

At our last meal together, he left me with a parting recommendation. "Tony," he said, "you need to write more songs like the hymns!" In spite of his obvious naiveteé on how hard it is to write songs, I thanked him for his suggestion. With a parting wave, he had left me a simple suggestion to write songs the church will sing for the next one hundred years! Why didn't I think of that? After all, hymns are only a collection of some of the greatest songs ever written in the history of the church.

I wish I had had the presence of mind to return the suggestion: "Thank you, and I would like to hear more messages with the depth and passion of Charles Spurgeon! Away with you now! I expect a first draft on my desk in six weeks!"

All kidding aside, I truly valued his insight and encouragement. But in defense of current songwriters, I would say it is the desire of serious writers of worship music to write songs the church would be singing for the next one hundred years! It's just easier said than done. The need is accurate and legitimate, but the mentors are few. I have written enough worship music (congregational) to know it is a specific gift, and I have a healthy respect for those who do it well. But there needs to be more teaching and impartation in this area.

The cumulative effect of conversations like these, prayer, study of God's Word, the insights gained from fathers (brothers and sisters), the many authors who have made deposits in me, the wrestling, and pressing into God have shaped my thoughts in the matter of writing and evaluating worship music. I, too, am concerned for the ground we have apparently ceded in our worship. We need to reevaluate our songs through a gospel lens. Our new songs need to reconnect the church to the gospel of Jesus Christ. This is the highest and most noble use of music and our gifts. The time is now. The world is straining for the reality of the gospel!

And, lest the young songwriters reading this feel that I have thrown them overboard, or have revealed myself as a member of the chronically *un-hip*, I would like to qualify my concern with a defense of some of the young writers of worship (and worshipers). In the years I have pastored and mentored some of these, there is much to be learned from the passion they bring to worship. It's not for lack of passion that I offer this observation, but a gentle, loving course correction in the content and scope of our priestlike role of writing and choosing good worship songs for our congregations; a return to elements of community (the "we" lyric); the value of teaching and educating our congregations through our songs.

"Where once we were in the age of the orator, we are now in the age of the artist! And, what we don't have them sing, they may never know."

—ANGLICAN BISHOP CRAY

Teaching and Educating through Our Songs

We need to reclaim the mandate to teach and educate in our songs, to help our congregations identify the object of our worship: God! Given the transient nature of our present-day, multinational, multicultural communities, we might be well-advised to identify the object of our worship as God, the father of Abraham, Isaac, and Jacob, and Jesus Christ the Messiah. If we are *not* more intentional in our song lyrics, we might possibly be providing a mere template for attendees to insert the god of their choosing.

How can we entice others into passionate worship with a God they know nothing about? We often leave our congregations to grasp and grope for a relationship they do not have, and with a God they do not know. Worship can be a wonderful compliment to the Word if we seize the opportunity to help our congregations connect the worship with the Word, to the grand narrative, to the great story of our redemption through Jesus, to the story of God the Creator, of God our Father! When we begin to write and choose songs that connect us with the bigger story, and our role in it, we will see more well-rounded, meaningful, passionate, and authentic worship.

My usual encouragement to worship writers (in workshops) is to write songs that eternalize and internalize the Word being taught from the pulpit in their individual churches. This is what we refer to as the *sound of the house*. What is God saying to *this congregation*, in *this season*, in *this community*? Sermons are not only a source of discovering God and hearing the gospel, but a great source for writing worship for your congregation.

The children of Israel passed their history and faith from generation to generation through songs; much of the tenants of the faith were entrusted to songs. Would we be willing to entrust such a critical burden on today's songs? Our forefathers did so because music contains the innate, God-infused quality of recall. We often forget what is spoken to us, but we are more likely to remember what we sing. This is one of the God-intended purposes for participatory, congregational music.

This concept can be easily demonstrated in a room full of old high school friends by recalling popular songs from their youth. Most can recall every line from their favorite songs of twenty or thirty years ago, and not miss a word. The exercise can be quite funny when someone recalls the lyrics wrongly, though. Like the old song "Forever in Blue Jeans" by Neil Diamond—to those who insisted it was a narrative song about Reverend Blue Jeans.

This element of recall, I believe, is a God-intended element of His creation of music—not simply to remind us of our past, but our future as well. It allows us a glimpse of heaven here on earth. In His grand design, God intended that music would transport us in the Spirit, from where we are, into His presence. Worship is where we reconcile our current station and circumstances, with the reality of the kingdom that awaits us. This is God's design and purpose for His creation of music and worship.

When we experience agreement between the worship and the Word, it lifts the whole worship experience. When we recognize and sing concepts we have been learning together, it intensifies the worship. Though they may not be able to name it, even the casual observer (those who walk into a church as a guest) will recognize authentic worship. It is undeniable. Authenticity is one of the highest standards you can aspire to, and one of the most critical elements of authentic worship is agreement. Agreement requires teaching and education.

When we combine God's creation of music (the vehicle) with the gospel (the content), which literally has the power to transform lives, we are cooperating with the kingdom of God by using music for its most powerful and created purpose.

Sam Storms once said, "God is not honored by heartless orthodoxy. Nor is he honored by joyful heresy. It isn't enough to think correctly or to feel passionately. To worship God truly we must have BOTH our heads aligned with truth AND our hearts on fire with love and joy inexpressible and full of glory! Only then shall we worship in a way that honors God and brings spiritual enrichment to our own souls."[8]

Hymns as a Template for Writing Worship

Hymns serve multiple purposes and fill many needs:

1. They are mostly theologically accurate.

2. They provide us a way to educate and teach our congregations.

3. They connect us with our church history and how our forefathers worshipped.

4. They connect us with the grand narrative and story of our redemption.

5. They assist in providing critical elements of gospel-centered worship.

6. They provide a great road map and template for young writers of worship.

---

8 Sam Storms, Theological Roundtable 2018, A Biblical Theology of Worship, Worship Kerygma Ministries, pg. 13. Permission granted.

I am not suggesting we should write new worship songs in the old hymn style (though there is much to be learned from their use of pace and content). I am mostly appealing to the value and content of the lyric that is so well represented in the old hymns. Great care and education were given to their representation of the gospel. The central ideas of the songs were gospel-centered. They were about Him and they celebrated Him, who He was, and what He did. They confront the listener and the congregation with the reality of who God is. They placed great confidence in the power of the gospel to transform people's lives.

In Acts, when Paul was time and again dragged into courts before kings, governors, magistrates, and religious leaders, all who had but one intention (to rid themselves of him), he, in risk of his own safety, preferred to trust his life to the propagation of the gospel. Paul placed supreme confidence in its power to transform. We, likewise, can trust our songs and our lyrics to the same confidence. Find the words, wrestle with the words, find new ways of communicating old truths. Trust the gospel!

The following is an excerpt of an article from a Theological Roundtable 2018 "Connecting our Worship to the Grand Narrative" Page 9 (A Seventy-Year Journey in Worship) by Dudley Hall:

> Though I was among those who welcomed the introduction of new songs and tunes in the 1970s, having grown tired of traditional hymns sung to old tunes, I recoiled then and still do at the presumption of those who make no room for the history of musical worship through hymns. It is almost like refusing to read church history or even like refusing to read theological works from the past. I state the obvious: Worship didn't start with this generation or with the Charismatic Movement. The value of the hymns that have survived through the years is how former believers expressed our common faith in different times. The "good" hymns featured sound biblical theology connected to the historical story of redemption. They magnified Jesus as the center of worship.[9]

---

9 Dudley Hall, Theological Roundtable 2018, A Seventy-Year Journey in Worship, Worship Kerygma Ministries, pg. 9. Permission granted.

I am concerned, not because I am older, but because I am more informed of the need of heart-deep, soul-washing worship. As a songwriter, I love a well-written song. And as a worship leader and pastor, I love a well-written song that feeds my flock and leads my congregation to the reality of the gospel.

There were considerable demands and expectations of songs in the history of the church. They were used to check off many boxes in the health and care of our souls, such as praise, thanksgiving, supplication, confession of sin, confession of faith, intercession, communion, to name a few. Many of today's worship songs fill these needs well. But as you might have learned through your examination of your current songs, you probably discovered there is ground to be reclaimed! We have abandoned much of the space the hymns occupied in a desire to be relevant and popular.

To Current Writers of Worship

My own appraisal of current worship songs reveals a need for:

1. Use lyrics that clearly establish we are talking about the God of Abraham, Isaac, and Jacob. We don't want to leave our congregations to grope for a vague, feckless, universal god, who bears no resemblance to the God that presides over all the events of time and existence; the God who shepherds our hearts and thoughts with sensitivity and intimacy.

2. Write songs with an intention of where it might be used in a worship song set. Is this a song of celebration? Or worship? Or communion? Or intimacy with God? Let your song rest in its created purpose to accommodate a specific function in the worship set. Resist the temptation of trying to capture every dynamic of a worship service in one song. The cumulative effect of too many of these songs in succession is like a roller-coaster effect. You will be a favorite among worship leaders if you learn to write songs with a specific sensitivity to the challenges of designing a worship set. We want our congregation to be able to experience a worship journey together in community.

A Shepherd's Thoughts

Songs will go places in the world you may never travel. They can facilitate communion with God for congregations around the world. They can comfort people at desperate times in the night and minister peace into troubled hearts.

I received a letter from a young lady who had lost her twenty-one-year-old twin sister to a congenital lung disease. She shared how she felt so abandoned and became very angry with God. Bitterness and resentment began building in her. She wrote:

> Then I was given a copy of a song you wrote: "If You Could Only See Me Now." I began listening to it late one night after everyone was asleep. I could not move. The tears poured. The words were exactly what I needed to hear. I played it again and again and again. I never cried so much. Oh, how I loved her. She was part of me. It is something every twin will tell you. But this night, I never felt closer to her, and closer to God. I don't know what you had to go through to write such a beautiful song, but God is using it to comfort those going through pain and loss. Thank you, Tony, and thank you, God!
>
> —Sharon Billings, MT

While I am climbing this long, beautiful hill called *sanctification*, I want to pause, turn around, and tell young songwriters who are sharing this creative journey that the most fulfilling, noble, profitable, and satisfying use of your creative gift is to write songs that allow others to experience and encounter God.

CHAPTER 11

Evaluating Team, Auditions, and On-Ramps

One of the most important responsibilities of worship leadership is the process of evaluating team members through auditions and on-ramps (the process to assist the leadership in determining a prospect's character, integrity, and maturity). This most often involves a new-members class and faithful attendance to a small group.

The time and effort you have invested in your vision, mission, and values will pay dividends in this process. Like putting on a pair of glasses, pass your decisions through the filter of your ministry principles. They will help you evaluate strategies to accomplish the mission and vision.

For instance, we had a vision to use a choir regularly as an expression of our worship because it checked off many of the boxes represented in our vision for worship ministry:

☑ Helping creatives find context for their gifts. We had a burden and conviction that when God gifted someone to sing, He intended for them to use their gift for the high and noble calling of serving the church.

☑ Influencing people with the gospel of Jesus Christ. A choir provides many more opportunities to influence people.

☑ Fulfilling the Great Commission by allowing more people access to gospel-centered community.

☑ Modeling worship for our congregation by reflecting authentic and effective worship.

The decision to use a choir (made easier by our vision) impacted our evaluation process because we were able to expand the number of vocalists we would be needing (for the purposes listed above). See how this works?

The evaluation process is not intended to identify perfection. Surprise! It will most assuredly reveal imperfection. My friend and pastor David Vestal said, "Don't make it harder to get on the worship team than it is to get into heaven." That is good counsel. The remedy for most issues that arise from the evaluation process is a spirit of humility. A humble individual will accept and respond to loving correction. Most issues we face can be resolved by humbling ourselves to God and others. When you diagnose offending behaviors or character flaws in others, don't miss the opportunities to invest grace, healing, and redemption. If there's any question whether our Father is invested in redemption, we need only to look in the mirror.

Our mandate as leaders is like the two sides of the same coin: while on one side we must protect our congregations by guarding our platform, on the other side we seek to redeem, rescue, and restore those who might unintentionally threaten our platform. When the evaluation reveals a character weakness, consider first what you can do to restore what the enemy may have stolen from this individual. But in the end, love and shepherd the individual enough to the value and freedom of humility.

We all need humility to face our issues.

As I have learned from experience, there are those who unfortunately are not willing to be pastored: "Faithful are the wounds of a friend" (Proverbs 27:6, ESV).

The Evaluation Process

Character and maturity are important aspects of all leadership. I recommend the audition process have two separate elements: an initial interview and a musical or technical audition. The following points are an example of the process I have used, but it's important that your process reflect your vision, mission, and values.

The Initial Interview

Begin the process with a rather informal interview to get to know the prospect. Ask many questions. Let them tell you who they are. Be conversational. Learn of their past, their families, their wives, their husbands, or their children. Begin the process of knowing them. Healthy relationships are all about knowing and being known.

This is a good time to present a summary of your process for joining the worship ministry. To those whose prior experience may not have been as deliberate, this will be a new experience, but healthy creatives will recognize and appreciate the differences.

As an illustration, allow me to relate this story. The professionals in the recording industry (e.g., musicians, engineers) like a recording session with a successful producer. By his mere presence, he raises the level of detail, expectation, and professionalism in the room. I have seen this effect firsthand, and sometimes even when the successful producer is not even producing.

I was producing a project in Nashville several years ago. We were tracking a song (laying the primary instruments: drums, bass, guitar, and keys), and we had reached the after-lunch slack, when the stomach begins borrowing neurons from the otherwise creative and focused brain. Good sessions usually leave the producer to simply choose from an abundance of creative ideas, but after lunch, the foot-long hoagie hush can leave the producer pulling focus and creativity up a hill. Then in walked a well-known record producer! I paused the session to greet my friend Greg Nelson, who had dropped in to see me and to see how the project was going. We visited for about five minutes, then Greg said, "I did not mean to interrupt. You are at work! Continue, I just wanted to sit in for a while."

I turned in my chair to reengage my session and realized I had somehow, during the pause, managed to regain total and complete creativity and focus. Of course, it wasn't me. This was the impact of having the attention of an award-winning producer in the room. This had transformed into an audition! I was getting a "gear" from my engineer and musicians I didn't even know they had.

What had changed was that Greg Nelson represented a standard of excellence that was demonstrably higher than my own. I knew and recognized this even in the moment and was glad for his presence to help us get over a common challenge of most recording days.

The culture and standard of excellence you're wanting to build begins in this initial interview by expanding the common definition of *excellence* to include not just musical excellence, but character and integrity. We, of course, want to identify unhealthy beliefs and attitudes, but this community is not looking to disqualify you. We want to prepare you to succeed, to serve others, to glorify God, and to build the kingdom of God.

Time is an important element of the vetting process. Relationships require the benefit of time. As a member of the congregation, I am more likely to enter into worship by following someone I know and trust (heart-deep). And, conversely, as a worship leader on the platform, I am much more effective when I know faces, stories, and testimonies of those I am leading in worship. In this way, the process will set up the new prospect for success!

We need to know those to whom we confer such trust. The evaluation process is designed to bring to light those who might have an unhealthy view of their gift. When the process exposes these unhealthy beliefs, we need to learn to love enough to help the prospect recognize the orphan spirit that informs them, and that their value as a son or daughter of God is not based upon their performance. They are sons and daughters first, who, because of the gospel, are free to use their gift to glorify God.

Generally speaking, this is not a time for rules, but relationships. We are not looking for reasons to reject people. They don't know what they don't know. It is likely no one has ever invested in them a context for their gift. I've seen this transition in practice, and not only in the context of music. It's like walking someone through a swamp to their first glimpse of the ocean. The gospel brings clarity to our gifts in ways we may never have imagined and reveals opportunities more vast than the oceans.

The initial interview should serve as a marker of sorts to determine spiritual maturity, humility, and patience. Here are questions you can ask:

- What is your vision for your gift and talent?

- If you were using your gift exactly as you desired, what would it look like?

- Do you like playing with other good musicians? Is it frustrating to play with musicians who are not as good as you?

- When singing with others, how do you help someone who is struggling with pitch?

- Do you have another gig besides playing at church? If yes, tell me about that experience.

- Our vision is to build as many worship teams as possible. Is that a challenge for you?

Manage expectations by educating the prospect on the process and requirements (and why you value the process and requirements). I promise, the healthy musicians will love this attention to detail. Musicians understand discipline and appreciate a thoughtful, secure environment in which to exercise their gift. An unhealthy musician will balk at a rigid on-ramp, seeing it as unnecessary or unreasonable. Learn to love these to wholeness; they eventually make great ambassadors for this kind of worship ministry and culture.

The Audition

Let's discuss auditions within the context of general worship ministry.

The Difficult Audition

While the difficult audition requires the most sensitivity, it also demands a change of direction when the prospect is clearly not musically or technically gifted. In this step of the process, we quickly learn words such as *talented*, *gifted*, and *excellent* can be relative terms. Every experienced worship pastor/ leader has had this kind of audition. It is, potentially, where we see the power of self-delusion on full display—and likely, the consequence of well-intended friends and family who prefer to avoid difficult conversations.

Particularly, singers who struggle with intonation, which can sometimes be corrected with learning proper breathing technique (with a professional vocal coach). But sometimes it indicates a disconnect in the ear's ability to hear a proper representation of the tone they are wanting to generate. This *cannot* be corrected.

While most auditions are pleasant, some require what I call *gentle truth*. In most of my conversations of this nature, I ask, "Has your experience with music been the source of frustration in the past?" Usually, the response comes with some emotions when they admit, "Yes, it has." Their body language and emotions usually indicate, "Finally, someone who cares enough to give me an honest opinion." And still, there are some prospects who will insist you are wrong, which we need to be secure enough to accept as a possibility. Nonetheless, it is your opinion that will determine their future participation, and all leadership comes with its share of challenges.

Because we value people more than their gift or talent, we, in a word, lovingly walk them toward their giftedness. On one such occasion, following one of these difficult auditions with a young lady, I asked in a staff meeting what were some of the greatest needs we currently had in our church. Several staff members said we had a desperate need for someone to oversee hospitality. When I mentioned this young lady's name as a candidate, everyone unanimously agreed. In time, she found her sweet spot of giftedness. Her success in serving our church community was so thoroughly successful that she decided to make hospitality her career. Win-win.

These precious people have labored under deception (maybe for many years), which has possibly hindered them in discovering their God-intended talent. It's why we invest time to help them find their true area of giftedness. This is more than walking them to the door—it's taking an active role in helping them discover, develop, and deploy in the body of Christ. God loves these people. They are not just auditioning for a band—they are vital members of God's family. In God's economy, nothing (and no one) is wasted.

The Vocal Audition

Having studied voice for many years, I have been on the other side of many auditions and know how nerve-racking they can be for the prospect. Here are a few recommendations that will improve your vocal audition process:

- Combine the initial interview with the audition. The opportunity to listen to the prospect fills a common need for all of us to be *known* and gives opportunity to settle the nerves the audition creates.

- Have more than one ear in the room to make an evaluation. Invite someone who represents the vision and values of the worship ministry and understands the spirit of the audition process.

- Have this additional person sing along with the prospect, as it makes the process less intimidating. And you can check the prospect's ear for hearing and singing parts.

- Don't make the audition long. If I spend thirty-five minutes with a prospect, thirty minutes is spent talking and listening and the remaining five minutes is an audition. This communicates a value: "We value the person more than the gift." This says, "We value *who you are* more than *what you might be able to do for us.*"

My actual audition looks something like this: I pick up my guitar and say, "Let's just sing a little bit together." I choose a song most everyone knows, such as "How Great Is Our God" (or any song the prospect is familiar with). I sing and invite everyone in the room to sing (not just the prospect). It removes the audition jitters, and we have some pretty good worship times too. Somewhere in the song, I will simply stop singing and listen to the voice of the prospect. I listen for:

1. intonation
2. control
3. power
4. vocal quality
5. harmonic capability

I ask my assistant to sing melody while the prospect finds a part to sing, to determine their ear for parts.

Considering the needs of a worship ministry, I categorize vocalists as:

- Those who can hear and sing melody and parts with little or no assistance.

- Those who can hear and sing melody only.

- Those who can hear and sing parts with some help.

- Those who can sing parts when standing next to someone singing the part (as in a choir).

- Those who have the vocal potential to lead a song in a worship service.

With the exception of those described in the "The Difficult Audition," I can usually find a place for vocalists, whether it be a potential worship leader, song leader, frontline vocalist, or choir member.

Note: It is helpful in any of the auditions to determine if the prospect is a trained musician (or can read music). This allows you to communicate to the prospect on multiple levels. Using an oversimplified example: Asking an untrained musician to sing the tenor line is generally accepted as the third above the melody. The trained musician might prefer the latter explanation for clarity.

The Instrumental Audition

There are a number of ways to audition instrumentalists (drums, bass, guitar, keys). Begin, of course, by giving them access to your songs and charts. Allow them a reasonable length of time to prepare before you arrange the audition. Also, if possible, allow them to choose a song they already know and are comfortable with. I prefer to hear what they can do when they're confident, not struggling to read a chart. Sight-reading is not a priority in this application. Understandably, this audition can also be intimidating. So, take time to allow them to settle into the moment, and ask questions that allow the musician to be known by the others. Let them share their experiences with music and their gift. In general, let them know they are in a welcoming and creative community that values them as a person first.

The two methods I have used for auditioning instrumentalists are:

1. Requesting them to attend a rehearsal. Allow time (ten to fifteen minutes) to sit in with the team. An added advantage in having the team present is consulting their opinions afterward.

Caution: Be mindful, as we are only seeking a snapshot of their gift. Don't allow the audition to get bogged down with unnecessary elements. A trained ear can assess their proficiency level rather quickly. Protect the heart of the prospect, regardless of their future participation on the platform as a rotating team member. They are still a valued member of God's family and deserving of our watch-care.

2. Taking them into the auditorium and feeding the song (prerecorded) through the monitor system and ask them to simply play along. I do this if a team is not readily available.

   The variations for setup are too numerous to list, as each instrument and musician may need a different setup. So, work to accommodate an environment that allows them to demonstrate their proficiency level.

   Avoid making your evaluation with just a solo performance. As impressive as it may be to hear a ten-minute blistering performance of a drum solo, there is an element of playing with a team (a band) that should be evaluated. Can they play with an awareness of tempo? Do they play with an awareness of what is going on around them? These deficiencies can be masked in a solo performance.

In general, make this a good experience. Remember, we are building an environment for people to discover their gifts, to develop their gifts, and to empower them to do the work of the ministry. It will, and should, look a little different for everyone. The prospect should at least leave the audition experience with a sense that they are in a loving and patient community of believers.

The Tech Artist Audition

Yes, there should be a tech audition, especially for audio technicians. I could be extremely facetious here. I spent twenty-five years navigating self-appointed soundmen. I have learned from experience that not everyone who aspires to such lofty positions of control (sarcasm implied) should be allowed to do so.

Allow me to relate an experience that illustrates this example to an absurd level. I was doing a concert one night and was fortunate to have a professional soundman with me. His credentials were such that I felt privileged to have him whenever he was available. Suffice it to say, this particular evening, he was not the least bit intimidated by the church sound system we were saddled with. As I was unloading my guitars and setting up, my soundman approached me and said quietly, "We have two problems."

Not feeling terribly concerned, as problems were common, I replied, "What, pray tell?"

He said, "First, the speaker on the right side of the auditorium is not working."

"Okay . . ." *Now I'm sitting down.*

"And, second, their house soundman is not going to let me behind the console."

Houston . . .

I said, "Okay, let's not lose our testimony over this. I'll go talk to him."

We approached the seventy-something-year-old soundman, who had both arms spread out over the console (so as to block any approaching interloper), when he said, "How can I help you?" Clearly, he was the captain of this ship, and we were but mere passengers on this perilous voyage. In spite of the fact we didn't have the ability to ever tack right.

I felt it best to address the "no sound in the right side of the auditorium" matter first. My choice of tact might somehow provide a collaborative focus that might promote a spirit of cooperation. So, using my powers of persuasion, I said, "Uh . . . did you know the speaker on the right side of your auditorium isn't working?"

To our amazement, he turned his head almost a full 180 degrees while *cupping his left ear* and said, "Huh?"

The problem became crystal clear. The soundman was deaf in his right ear. Bears repeating: the soundman was deaf in his right ear. How would *he* know the speaker on the right side of the auditorium was not working?

I really did want to stay and move on to our second issue, but I knew that anything more I might have said would have been preceded with a very disrespectful guffaw. I bit my lower lip and dismissed myself to the foyer. I left my capable soundman to navigate these complex waters.

My professional soundman was eventually able to convince the house soundman of his worth by fixing their speaker issue, to which he was subsequently welcomed behind the console. He saved the evening with his great attitude and aptitude.

After the concert (on the way to the hotel), my soundman related the rest of the story, which sent me into a convulsion again. The reason the elderly soundman was relegated to running sound was because, when in the choir, he lost hearing in his right ear. The other choir members then started complaining about his intonation issues, so their remedy was to let him run the house sound system. I can imagine the following conversation: "Hey, I know how we can get him out of the choir. Let's put the deaf guy on the soundboard!"

Funny as this is, it is not uncommon when we have no reasonable audition process for tech.

So what *does* a technical audition look like? Much the same way we vet worship team members, we are most certainly looking for competency, but also character, humility, integrity, and faithfulness. Begin this process (again) with a simple interview: cloak it in a coffee, lunch, or any impromptu setting that will promote a candid conversation. Here are a few questions to ask:

- Do you have experience with audio, lighting, visuals, or operating a camera (whatever their expressed area of interest might be)? Was the experience related to your profession, or was it as a volunteer? (The response could lead you to helpful discovery.)

- In your previous experience, did you work as an individual or with a team? What was that experience like? Did you learn anything new? (The question is intended to determine if they are teachable, or a team player. Remember, we are not looking for ways of rejecting people, but sometimes these casual conversations reveal an orphan spirit that becomes more important to address than any immediate need of the tech team. Putting an unhealthy person in this role can make matters worse. We want a healthy, whole team member who is free to offer their gifts in a loving and accepting environment. Time, prayer, and relationship are the remedy!)

- Explain the on-ramp process defined by the elders and leaders, and ask their response to the process. This might give you an indication of their spiritual maturity.

Tech team auditions should follow this pattern:

- I do, you watch.

- You ask questions, I answer.

- I teach, you learn.

- Then last, you do, and I watch.

Patience, maturity, and faithfulness can only be evaluated over time. Some things just can't be rushed. Don't compromise the integrity of the culture by allowing someone to circumvent the process (or fast-track a prospect). You may not think anyone is watching, but you can damage the culture you've worked so hard to cultivate with little compromises. You can cheapen the contributions of others by not valuing the sacrifices they have made to fill their role faithfully and responsibly.

Additional thought: Most tech roles are teachable, given time and training. The exception is audio (sound). In my opinion, musicians make better sound techs (not an absolute). But when you consider the whole, the soundman is the ultimate musician in the room. He has control of every instrument and voice on the platform. He should approach the console as an instrument that can impact the dynamic of the whole worship service (good and bad). But they must be actively, musically, and spiritually engaged in the worship service. This requires spiritual maturity. And spiritual maturity takes time to evaluate.

We will discuss more about the expanding role and responsibilities of tech in Chapter 12.

The On-Ramp

Worship ministries, more so than other ministries in the church, attract some who struggle with performance issues. I mean, how many ushers have you seen complaining they have not been invited to "ush" in six weeks? On-ramps are a great way to help leadership identify those struggling with an unhealthy orphan spirit. Time spent in a small group will often expose these subtleties.

The spirit of the on-ramp is not intended to find weakness and fault in every prospect, but to help leadership vet those who might need additional pastoring before releasing them to serve the worship ministry. Be careful of the tendency to become too rigid and legalistic about your on-ramp. While we need to honor the process (and our vision and values), we want to remember it's not about rules, but relationships.

This should serve as an example of an on-ramp process:

1. The prospect and their gift are discovered.

2. The initial interview should determine character and spiritual maturity. In order to manage expectations (of both parties), give them a copy of the Worship Team Handbook (and any social media contract, which I recommend) for their own consideration. Inform them that attendance of your membership class and participation in a small group is a prerequisite of their involvement in the worship ministry. (Quality of relationship should be the priority over a specified amount of time.)

3. The audition can happen any time after the initial interview (sometimes in the same meeting or within a few weeks). If the audition was satisfactory, let them know your thoughts and impressions of the audition and whether they met your current proficiency level (be encouraging, but noncommittal on a final decision), and that you need to wait for them to fulfill the prerequisite requirements. (When the audition does not go well, review "The Difficult Audition.")

4. Within two to three months, consider following up with their small-group leader and verify attendance and participation. If there are no warning flags, invite them to observe a rehearsal and meet a few team members.

5. At the three- or four-month mark (assuming everyone still has a peace about the prospect), begin a more regular conversation and invite them to the platform during a rehearsal (to sing

or play their instrument). Toward the end of this period (sometimes needs-driven), invite the prospect to the platform for a weekend to get a feel for the rehearsal commitment, preparation level of the team, and rhythm and pace of the services. (Note: Before the weekend rehearsal starts, announce to the team that the prospect will be joining them but is still in the evaluation process. In order to redirect any awkwardness, say, "Our prospect will be *auditioning us* this weekend, so be on your best behavior!")

When the Prospect Has Been Approved

When a prospect has completed the prerequisite class and participation in small groups, has met the minimum proficiency level audition, and there is consensus among the leadership, inform the prospect they are officially a member of your worship ministry.

When the time is appropriate, make a big deal about it. This is a significant trust we are conferring upon this person, and they have been approved! Promote them among the team—maybe introduce them to the team at their first official in-rotation rehearsal as the newest member. Bring everyone a cupcake! Carve out time to share what you like most about them. It will be a special moment to remember, not only for the new member but the current team. You are demonstrating value for the current team and the new member. This kind of celebration will assist in building your worship ministry culture. You just can't overdo this. It is said, "You value what you celebrate, and you celebrate what you value!"

As a matter of practice, look for every opportunity to affirm team members (remember tech!) and how valuable they are to the team. Call out the godly character you observe in them. They will begin to reflect the way you value them.

Final Thoughts Regarding the Evaluation Process

Here are a few additional thoughts regarding the evaluation process that are important but often overlooked:

1. Social media (Facebook, Instagram, Twitter) has become a popular and highly visible platform for communicating and influencing others. Many churches and Christian organizations have wisely educated their leadership of the responsibility of a consistent testimony and the importance of a good reputation on any platform (be it a physical platform at church or an online social media platform). I recommend a social media contract be a part of your handbook and covenant for all participants of your worship ministry.

2. Caution regarding the audition process: Remind the leadership involved in the evaluation process to honor the dignity of the process by guarding their conversation with prospects; remind them not to use verbiage that would indicate their shoe-in participation until the evaluation is complete, and until unanimous consent among the leaders is confirmed. Be familiar with the on-ramp and be patient to allow the process to work in the best interest of the church and the prospect. Carefully manage expectations! Keep in mind the dual role: to guard our platform, and to lovingly set people up to succeed.

A Shepherd's Thoughts

In my years as a recording artist traveling much of the world and doing concerts, I met many talented musicians and artists. Many of whom were not using their gifts in any appreciable way. The cumulative effect of this twenty-five-year experience left me wondering if we (as the church) are missing an opportunity to provide creatives a context and purpose for their gifts.

In thirteenth and fourteenth centuries, the church commissioned many of the great works of art (including many famous paintings). These works assisted the public (many who could not read Scripture) to visualize the stories and characters of the Bible in hopes of inspiring the congregations to greater devotion and ultimately salvation. The church was heavily invested in art (more than just music). The church provided a context and purpose for creatives. This clarity provided inspiration when they connected their gift with a divine purpose.

Some of the most successful creatives (who have created excellent works of staggering proportions) are yet some of the most miserable examples of fulfillment and success, because their gifts lack context and connection with their intended purpose.

Building a healthy worship ministry today requires breaking down the worldly, counterfeit definitions of *excellence* that have crept into our worship culture. The gospel informs us that excellence has everything to do with the heart, the character, and the integrity of the artist.

Love those God entrusts to your care enough to help them make this connection with the eternal, divine purpose God intended for their gifts and talents.

CHAPTER 12

The changing Face of Tech in church culture

Information technology (IT) has become essential in church culture today. Most churches, pre-COVID, were already providing an online presence for their Sunday services. But in 2020, COVID forced the remaining few holdouts into the *virtual church service* (of necessity)—not only a means of providing a Sunday service, but as means of conducting small groups (e.g., Zoom, GoToMeeting).

In the past, tech existed primarily for the audio and visual experience on Sunday morning, but it's now an important element in projecting the *face* of the ministry. Maintaining and fostering a good testimony in the community has always been very important, but now tech has become a key element of projecting and communicating that good testimony. This is why the ministry principles of vision, mission, and values should equally inform your technology; it's also a good argument for keeping tech under the watch-care of the worship ministry. The role and responsibilities of tech are so closely related it makes sense to combine the two under one ministry oversight.

One of the foundational responsibilities of a worship pastor is to be keenly aware of elements that are (or could be) potentially distracting to the congregation's worship experience. This has come to include the online worship experience. A poor broadcast of the service (i.e., audibly, visibly, technically) would certainly fall under the category of *distracting*.

As somewhat a disclaimer, my reason for discussing the changing face of technology in church is not intended to suggest I am advocating for the replacement of the live church service. I am not. Nor am I remotely suggesting the idea of *virtual discipleship* as an adequate substitute for one-on-one, face-to-face discipleship. Hebrews 10:24–25 (ESV) says, "And let us consider how to stir up one another to love and good works, not neglecting to meet together, as is the habit of some, but encouraging one another, and all the more as you see the Day drawing near." These virtual alternatives are, in fact, poor substitutions for live fellowship. We need the proximity of other believers (the indwelling Holy Spirit) for encouragement and edification. Virtual church does not fill this need! And its use should be the exception, not the rule.

While we should be vigilant of technology that would distract us from our commission, we certainly need to be willing to embrace technologies that aid in the effectiveness of that commission. For instance, today we seldom see churches without microphones. The microphone has made it possible to host much larger audiences, not to mention an important element in recording messages and music that are used to broadcast our messages worldwide. In this way, we embrace technology that improves our ability to share the gospel.

Servants Only Need Apply

The most significant challenge in finding good tech team members is the balance between competency and servanthood. It's probably better to choose your tech team from a pool of servant-minded individuals rather than from a pool of technically minded individuals. This is not intended to disparage tech artists—it's simply a rule of averages. Those whose temperament has prepared them to be excellent in the technical arts will tend to see issues as more black and white.

You will be better served to find those whose first filter is that of a servant (grace), who also has an aptitude for the technical arts and is willing to be trained. Remember, training is a perfectly acceptable method and process for building a tech team.

Consider this: because the technical disciplines are becoming more complex, each event/meeting requires staffing with competent personnel. Your tech personnel will most likely be the first to arrive and the last to leave (and in many instances will be your church representatives). These individuals should be competent, cordial, heart-deep in your fellowship, and most of all servants.

Your priority when vetting tech artists is to ask, Are they teachable? This, frankly, is a priority when I am asked to build a team for any endeavor. Those who think they have little or nothing to learn from another person or experience will quickly find themselves at the end of their own resources and knowledge. If there's anything I have learned from being around successful creative people, it's their amazing capacity to absorb. Their knowledge base is ever-expanding. This is a common posture among people who are labeled successful. They watch, they listen, they absorb, and they integrate all they learn into their own unique combination and expression of skill sets.

Technology changes constantly, which means that technology in our churches will change. As with our worship teams, we want to teach the tech artist how to find a context and purpose for their gift. When unhealthy attitudes and beliefs surface with the tech team, they, too, will need pastoring. The quality we most value in our tech team is not perfection, but a competent humility that manifests itself in a willingness to learn and serve.

Paid or Volunteer Tech Director? And Digital or Analog?

These two questions belong in the same discussion. The answer to one depends on the other. Here is the objective: Make sure the competency level of your personnel matches your technology. Most issues regarding media and tech arise from the confusion of not having answered these questions. I will unpack some of the challenges and offer clarity and solutions to this problem.

First, ask three questions of your tech needs:

1. What is your vision for media and technology?

   The answer to this is limited often by the size of your church (and thus the budget). Regardless of your church's current tech status, this mental exercise is useful for determining and considering needs, and at least helpful in casting vision for your church leadership.

2. What applications do you need/want your technology to serve?

   Live sound, lighting, and visuals for your services (this is obviously a foundational need, but it should be accounted for, as it will make demands on your tech resources).

   Online streaming (prior to the COVID-19 pandemic, this was not essential, but circumstances have made it more important and, of necessity, our world has become more accepting of the virtual option).

   Audio and visual recording and editing (requires many different skill sets, such as pre- and post-production, software, graphics, etc.).

3. What is the status of your tech personnel currently? Are they qualified and proficient to operate the current tech systems? Will they be qualified and proficient to match the future vision of the church systems?

The answers to these questions might provide some clarity. The saying "A chain is only as strong as its weakest link" is appropriate here. You may have a big vision for media and tech, but you may not have the budget or personnel to execute the vision.

Most new technology is digital, and digital has its advantages, but it does not mean digital is superior to analog. Many churches don't have qualified people who can operate and maintain digital systems. Even seasoned IT can be confused when asked to convert their knowledge to digital audio and visual systems, as they are somewhat unique and different applications. A digital system requires not only an IT mentality, but a specific working knowledge of audio and visual application. Let's face it: backing up, storing, and recalling settings (common functions in digital systems) require a different skill set and temperament. Unless you have dependable audio and visual technical counsel, you might choose analog (still a viable option). Most volunteers can (with a minimal amount of training) learn an analog system; thus, training and maintaining a team of volunteers becomes more manageable.

I am not opposed to digital systems in churches, but often it's a short list of volunteers who have the patience and aptitude to learn, maintain, and run the systems. In time, the demands on that short list of people becomes unreasonably burdensome (especially if they are volunteering). To help you in your decision-making, here are pros and cons to consider:

1. Digital pros and cons:

    a. Pros: Cleaner audio signals (lower noise floor); scene and channel storage and recall; minimal physical space required; portability (mixing apps, personal mixers).

    b. Cons: Qualified personnel (fewer techs); training curve; repairs (non-modular).

2. Analog pros and cons:

    a. Pros: Easier to train; repairs to modular console less disruptive; problems with signal flow are diagnosed more easily.

    b. Cons: Noisy (more susceptible to interference); no scene and channel storage or recall; requires more physical space and more cabling.

I'm sometimes asked, "We are beyond the question of analog versus digital. We are heavily invested in digital. Should we pay for a qualified media and tech director?"

My short answer is yes! Let the required output of the technology dictate whether you hire part time or full time.

First, a question: If you invest a considerable amount of money in an airplane, should you pay someone to fly it? This might be an extreme illustration, but if you have an expensive, complex sound system, with complex visuals software and projection systems, cameras and editing needs (for live and recorded feeds) as many churches do now, you need to have a qualified, dependable, paid employee (part time or full time) to oversee and maintain the systems—not unlike a professional pilot. It's simply a reality of the changing times we live in. As we discussed previously, much of the *face* and communications of the church are executed virtually today.

If you choose the digital option, or if the demands are such that your church no longer has an option, the ideal structure is to find a faithful, qualified, patient, pastoral, empowering media and tech director who can build a dynamic, servant-hearted, Jesus-loving tech ministry. I understand . . . it's a tall order. You can sometimes streamline and combine this role if you have someone among your worship leadership who has this gear.

My first memory of Jon Ford was of a twelve-year-old young man hanging around our youth sound console. His family had served our worship ministry at every point of service (worship leaders, musicians, tech, pastors, etc.). It was apparent Jon would be following his family's example by immersing himself in our worship culture. Jon absorbed everything, including manuals. He embraced the vision and the spirit of our worship ministry. He became my right hand in every sense. He became the standard by which I measured our team (worship and tech).

Jon not only served tech needs, but he was proficient at several instruments. So, he often played an instrument while simultaneously instructing tech on which buttons to push. We had four sound systems and a recording studio in our building, all of which Jon knew better than anyone. He was a true utility person. But what was most impressive was he did it all with the heart of a servant. My most pressing challenge became trying to protect him from burnout from those who might take advantage of him by assuming upon his time. Jon became indispensable, and we began paying him.

Jon is now married (to his lovely wife Michelle), and they serve another fellowship in the Dallas area. When I asked him what his new fellowship knew of his multiple giftings, he replied, "Nothing yet!" We had a good laugh. But when Jon chooses to engage, they will find a well-rounded, multi-talented, gospel-centered servant. Jon was certainly a blessing to me, but he is the product of a gospel-centered worship culture that will serve and influence the kingdom of God for generations.

If your vision or current reality is to serve all the applications we have introduced here, you need to get your staff and leadership over the hump of the necessity of recognizing that a paid media and technical director is now *essential personnel*. It is a reality of digital. Lead pastors, associate pastors, small-groups pastors, youth pastors, worship pastors, clerical assistants, and yes, paid media and technical directors are all essential.

A Shepherd's Thoughts

All that being understood: I am neither for nor against digital technology. My intent is to unpack a common source of frustration that often accompanies the implementation of new digital technologies into a mostly volunteer servant base. When making a decision for your church regarding media and tech, it's helpful to have a full appreciation of the cost, which is not just an equipment investment, but also a personnel investment.

If you are a small church, and you don't have these demands (or the budget), or the personnel to staff these new technologies, consider investing in an analog system and count yourself blessed (until the demands become such that you need to invest in a bigger and more robust system). And when the season for change comes, move forward with an informed understanding of the cost of the decision.

CHAPTER 13

From the Heart of a Worship Shepherd

This book was truly a labor of love—a love for those who faithfully seek to serve the church, to glorify God, and to build the kingdom of God; a love for worship leaders and pastors who are often left to pioneer their own definitions of a faithful ministry of worship; a love for God's church and His people; and a love for the gospel of Jesus Christ. I place great confidence and trust in the gospel of Jesus Christ. The gospel is not only a historical and biographical account of the life and ministry of Jesus, but it is a template and filter through which we see and experience life. The implications of the gospel not only inform our personal lives and ministries, but they act as a portal through which order and hope are restored to mankind.

In 2003, the gospel transformed my world. It challenged my personal walk, my ministry, my relationships, and the way I related to music. My daily tasks changed, my goals for life were changed, my understanding of ministry changed, and several unhealthy aspects of my own career choices were challenged.

This new reality in my life crystalized one day when walking into my office. I rounded the corner of my desk and glanced a look at my guitar sitting on a stand next to my chair. My guitar was always within arm's length for any quick inspiration, like the comfort of an old friend. What surprised me this day was what I did when I glanced at that old friend. I shook my head in disappointment. I had to stop myself and think, *Where did* that *come from? When did my guitar begin to represent disappointment to me?*

This was a guitar my father bought me for my seventeenth birthday—a vintage Martin D35 (with a Brazilian rosewood three-piece back). When did my guitar begin to represent anything other than joy and comfort to me? What had happened? I used to go into my room to play and write songs for hours, for the pure joy of singing, playing, and creating. What had changed?

By 2003, I had had enough successes to feel validated in my career. As a songwriter, I was a published writer and several major-label artists had recorded my songs. As an artist, I had several songs in the nation's Top 20 Christian charts. I was doing enough live appearances to provide for my family. By most standards among creatives in Nashville, I was successful. But I didn't feel that way. I had a curious, nagging sense I was missing something. What was happening?

God was beginning to reorder my priorities.

I prayed earnestly for God to restore my joy and love for music (and my guitar!). I felt something had been taken from me; no one else knew, but I was in a personal crisis. I did the only thing I knew to do and opened God's Word on the matter. I was a Christian and I knew God's Word provided comfort and wisdom for me personally, but would it speak to my career choice? Would it provide clarity to my expectations of fulfillment and success in music? Would it help me understand why my guitar began representing *failure?*

I began a word study of all things music-related in Scripture. God met me that day and many days after. My pursuit of music became a pursuit of the heart of God. "If any of you lacks wisdom, let him ask of God, who gives to all liberally and without reproach, and it will be given to him" (James 1:5, NKJV).

My study revealed how God used music in Scripture:

- As a means of comfort (regarding Saul): I Samuel 16:16 (NKJV) says, "Let our master now command your servants, who are before you, to seek out a man who is a skillful player on the harp. And it shall be that he will play it with his hand when the distressing spirit from God is upon you, and you shall be well."

- As a means of refreshing and healing: I Samuel 16:23 (NKJV) says, "And so it was, whenever the spirit from God was upon Saul, that David would take a harp and play it with his hand. Then Saul would become refreshed and well, and the distressing spirit would depart from him."

- As a ministry to God: II Samuel 6:5 (NKJV) says, "Then David and all the house of Israel played music before the LORD on all kinds of instruments of fir wood, on harps, on stringed instruments, on tambourines, on sistrums, and on cymbals." I Chronicles 13:8 (NKJV) says, "Then David and all Israel played music before God with all their might, with singing, on harps, on stringed instruments, on tambourines, on cymbals, and with trumpets."

- Celebrating God's attributes and virtues: II Chronicles 5:13 (NKJV) says, "Indeed it came to pass, when the trumpeters and singers were as one, to make one sound to be heard in praising and thanking the LORD, and when they lifted up their voice with the trumpets and cymbals and instruments of music, and praised the LORD, saying: 'For He is good, For His mercy endures forever,' that the house, the house of the LORD, was filled with a cloud."

- Praising the Lord: Psalms 33:2 (NKJV) says, "Praise the LORD with the harp; Make melody to Him with an instrument of ten strings."

- As inspiration into battle: Joshua 6:4–5 (NKJV) says, "And seven priests shall bear seven trumpets of rams' horns before the ark. But the seventh day you shall march around the city seven times, and the priests shall blow the trumpets. It shall come to pass, when they make a long blast with the ram's horn, and when you hear the sound of the trumpet, that all the people shall shout with a great shout; then the wall of the city will fall down flat. And the people shall go up every man straight before him."

- Announcing and preparing the people for the presence of God: I Chronicles 15:28 (NKJV) says, "Thus all Israel brought up the ark of the covenant of the LORD with shouting and with the sound of the horn, with trumpets and with cymbals, making music with stringed instruments and harps."

My study of God's Word regarding music revealed this common thread: The highest use of God's creation of music is to represent, announce, or prepare God's people for God's presence; and the highest, most noble calling for creatives is to cooperate with God's design for music by serving others, glorifying God, and building the kingdom of God.

A gospel-centered worship service checks off all these boxes.

Worship is the purest, most authentic use of God's creation of music, and the highest calling God can place upon a creative is to serve the church.

I would desire that all creatives discover this truth (saved and unsaved). All of God's creation testifies of God. In Luke 19:40, the Pharisees believed it was blasphemous for the people to be worshipping Jesus because they did not recognize His deity. Jesus answered, "I tell you, if these were silent, the very stones would cry out" (ESV).

Many creatives have never experienced the true power of music as when it is combined with the transformative power of the gospel. This has become my life's passion: loving, pastoring, mentoring, shepherding, and fathering creatives to this truth. The fulfillment, encouragement, and validation we seek as creatives flows out of this understanding!

A Word to the Artists

It's always important for me to include my brothers and sisters in the music industry (Christian and secular). I'm not discounting the countless contributions of great songs and recordings that are a wonderful testimony of the excellence of His creation of music. I spent most of my adult life writing these songs and chasing them around the world (in concerts).

I am, though, representing that congregational singing (worship) is the highest use of the creation of music, and to serve His church by providing opportunity for holy fellowship and communion with God, through music, is the highest use of our musical gifts.

Some may gain celebrity status and have other, larger platforms (nationwide or worldwide), but unless one establishes their foundation within gospel-centered community, they will not experience the fulfillment, encouragement, validation, and context God intended for their gift. This is God's order. These are the people who *when you fall* will pick you up, brush you off, remind you who you are, and set you back on your journey. This community becomes a filter through which you evaluate and process your failures and successes.

Let me demonstrate this principle. I had polio when I was a child. I wore a brace on my right leg until I was ten years old. I had a series of corrective surgeries throughout my childhood, and now the only remaining visible evidence is a limp. This handicap had an enormous impact on my life, but it did *not* overwhelm me. Because I had a family who treated me no differently than any other family member. I had the same responsibilities and accountabilities as my other brothers and sisters, but also, all the advantages of proportion to my life challenges and experiences. This provided balance to my life. My family was the foundation (or community) that allowed for my successes.

So, whether you serve the church through worship ministry, or your unique gifts provide you other (larger) platforms, your foundation should still be the church. A mature understanding of gifts and talents acknowledges the foundation of gospel-centered community. Everything flows out of this; it is what gives depth, breadth, and meaning to our art and ministries. Creativity, authenticity, and power flows through gospel-centered community.

A Shepherd's Thoughts

My wife and I like to watch Disney and Pixar animations. We marvel at the creativity and excellence of the new technologies and productions. As a songwriter, I listen to the music for pretty melodies, creative lyrics, and good chord progressions. We sometimes talk about these productions for months! We love to watch things done with excellence. We might even watch it a second or third time, but eventually the wonder wears off. Something new captures our attention and becomes the new standard of excellence. The wonder of excellent songs comes and goes, the impact of great productions comes and goes, but they have never transformed my life.

One night in 1975, in a small Baptist church in Havre, Montana (thirty-five miles south of the Canadian border), I heard a song called "O How He Loves You and Me." Something in that simple song touched my heart deeply, and my world changed. That was the night I was saved. I invited Jesus into my life. The song was not cloaked in a multimillion-dollar production, nor did it have any of the advantages of the latest creative technologies. And yet, it changed my life for *eternity*.

What was the difference? The gospel. The transformational power of the gospel.

Let's Worship Together

In my spirit I am saddled, my canteen is full, the wind is at my back, and I will head someday into that great sunset in the sky! But until the Lord calls me home, I am content to impart the download God has made in me. After all, what a waste if a young worship leader or pastor had to start from where I did. I would much rather give someone my shoulders on which to stand to begin their journey. Why would they have need to learn the same lessons and make the same mistakes I did?

I am not opposed to institutions, seminaries, or schools of worship, but I feel something is lost when we seek remedies designed for a one-size-fits-all output. I prefer individual discipling that is more adept at weaving the individual giftings, callings, and talents into a unique worship expression and more effective for discovering the sound of the house (for individual churches).

In our COVID reality, we discovered a few positives. Among these is the comfort level with online meetings and communications. I have led a small group for many years, and 2020 forced us along with countless millions to online meetings. We resisted this forced alternative as an inefficient, ineffective substitute to face-to-face, one-on-one discipling—not to mention the impossibility of leading worship online (what a train wreck!). But it did offer an intriguing opportunity to connect with worship leaders worldwide (one-on-one or in groups), to provide help for those who need a shepherding worship mentor to be able to discuss challenges that are unique to worship ministry. Whereas most churches cannot afford the luxury of a campus worship pastor to oversee worship leaders and ministries, an extra local worship shepherd (mentor) might be more financially realistic.

It is my intention to engage a limited number of churches to provide encouragement, wisdom, and guidance to worship leadership (the kind represented in this book), such as:

- Weekly online worship meetings with leaders. Initially one-on-one, with a goal of graduating to a worship leader group meeting (five to ten other worship leaders from other churches).

- Access to counsel. A campus visit for needs-driven meetings with lead pastors, elders, worship teams, etc.

A worship shepherd might be a luxury to one church, but it might be a blessing to many churches. If you or your fellowship would benefit from this arrangement, I would be glad to talk with you about a worship mentor relationship through these methods.

Following are additional benefits to a mentor relationship:

- Work with songwriters (songwriting and congregational songwriting). Visit tonyelenburg.com for information.

- Worship EP: I will guide your team through the process of writing, recording, and releasing an EP. (I have a BBA in business administration with an emphasis on the music industry from Belmont University in Nashville, Tennessee, and over forty years of experience in the process of recording music.)

Acknowledgments

My wife, Cindy, has been a constant companion in all my adventures for forty-two years. Some of those adventures have been successful and immensely rewarding, and yet others not so. She has managed to be supportive and positive through them all. I wish to express my love to my wife of forty-two years. Also, my children, Taylor, Tana Kaye, and Victoria, for their contributions of giving a father to the demanding ministry of the gospel.

One Sunday morning, I was sitting (somewhat anonymously) in a church service in Vancouver, Washington. I sat about ten rows from the platform in the second of three services they offered that morning. Toward the end of the worship set, a young lady approached the microphone to lead the congregation in the last song of the set. I overheard a lady behind me say, "I love it when this girl leads." Words are not sufficient to describe the overwhelming sense of thankfulness that swept over me. What was an insignificant comment from the lady was, to me, a culmination of many years of investment of leading worship into my daughter, and it was being confirmed to me through a simple unsolicited compliment. It assured me I wasn't just a biased, proud father gushing over his daughter (though I am all those things). Few would know the hours Tori invested in listening, asking, and absorbing, or the deep places she has mined in her own heart to settle the issues of her calling. She now is part of a worship leadership team at a church in Belton, Texas (Crossroads Church), where she and her husband have since moved. Thank you, Tori, for letting me share and watch your journey. I am proud of you and I love you.

David Vestal is, and has been, one of my dearest friends for almost forty years. He has served as a board member for my ministry for most of those years. Our relationship has survived many changes in dynamic, such as the year he became my pastor when we moved to Dallas to attend Lighthouse Christian Fellowship in Prosper, Texas (where David was the founding pastor). I was invited to the platform soon after I arrived and was eventually asked to lead and pastor the worship ministry. Much of this book, and the insight to building and pastoring a worship ministry, was the result of David's investment in me. I wish to thank David and his wife Dana, and the wonderful brothers and sisters of Lighthouse, for allowing me to see that I had another gear, not just as a songwriter and concert/recording artist, but as a pastor.

This book is dedicated posthumously to my good friend Charlie Chivers. He was a very special friend. I will miss him (but only for a while). I met Charlie at a critical point in my life. He walked me to understanding regarding my own disability, and his ministry lives on in many of my songs. Our families grew up and vacationed together. So many rich, rich memories (and funny ones).

Charlie's heart beat for Special Touch Ministry (a ministry to the disabled community). Charlie and Debbie will both be honored in heaven for their life dedication to those with disabilities—a people group that is often dismissed and overlooked. For more information, visit the website: specialtouch.org.

Tony Elenburg

Tony Elenburg is a 40-year music industry veteran who left Nashville to help build one of the fastest growing churches in North Dallas. He served as the executive worship pastor for Lighthouse Christian Fellowship in Prosper, Texas. As a songwriter and recording artist, Tony and his songs have been heard on national Christian radio, with ten Top 20 hits, as well as numerous songs recorded by artists such as The Little River Band, Orleans, and Steven Curtis Chapman. These experiences birthed a deep passion in Tony to invest a gospel context into musicians so they can be fulfilled in their gifts and embrace the value of the high and noble calling of serving the church. He lives in Prosper, Texas, with his wife Cindy and is the author of *A Worship Shepherd.*

Connect with the Author

tonyelenburg.com
Instagram.com/tdelenburg
Facebook.com/RioVidaMusic
tony@riovidamusic.com

Leave a Review

If you enjoyed reading *A Worship Shepherd*, will you consider leaving a review on your platform of choice? Reviews help self-published authors find more readers like you.

www.ingramcontent.com/pod-product-compliance
Lightning Source LLC
Chambersburg PA
CBHW020545160726
47991CB00002B/589